Assembling a Collaborative Project Team

Practical Tools including Multidisciplinary Schedules of Services

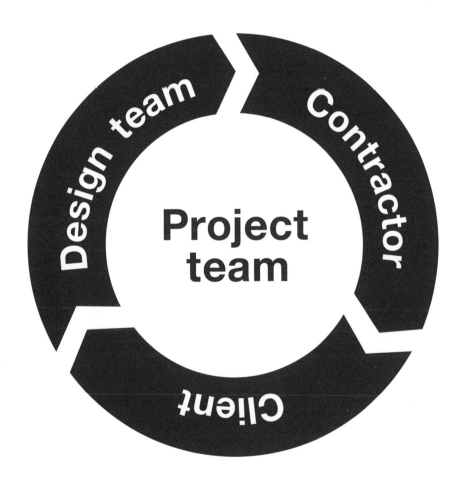

RIBA 🏛 **Publishing**

www.ribaplanofwork.com

© Dale Sinclair, 2013

Published by RIBA Publishing, 15 Bonhill Street, London EC2P 2EA

ISBN 978 1 85946 497 7

Stock code 80461

The right of Dale Sinclair to be identified as the Author of this Work has been asserted in accordance with the Copyright, Designs and Patents Act 1988.

British Library Cataloguing in Publication Data
A catalogue record for this book is available from the British Library.

Commissioning Editor: Sarah Busby

Designed by www.darkhorsedesign.co.uk

Printed and bound by W&G Baird Ltd in Great Britain

While every effort has been made to check the accuracy and quality of the information given in this publication, neither the Author nor the Publisher accept any responsibility for the subsequent use of this information, for any errors or omissions that it may contain, or for any misunderstandings arising from it.

RIBA Publishing is part of RIBA Enterprises Ltd.

www.ribaenterprises.com

Foreword

When the RIBA Plan of Work was first created in 1963, it set out the tasks to be undertaken by the design team at each project stage and subsequent versions have continued in this vein. The RIBA Plan of Work has evolved over time to reflect changes in project team organisation and construction delivery models.

The RIBA Plan of Work 2013 takes this evolution a step further by addressing changes in procurement and making an important shift in emphasis from the design team to the project team as a whole, reflecting the new professional and information landscape and acknowledging the cultural and contractual changes that have taken place in recent years.

Assembling a Collaborative Project Team keeps the momentum of the new RIBA Plan of Work driving forward by offering cutting-edge guidance on how project teams are procured and assembled as well as analysing the entities that comprise the project team: the client, the design team and the contractor. It builds on the processes set out in the *Guide to Using the RIBA Plan of Work 2013* and provides further tools and techniques to assist in the team-building process. It also clarifies the importance of the first two stages of the RIBA Plan of Work 2013, explaining their role in giving a project the best possible start.

By facilitating the formation of collaborative project teams, the RIBA will act as a catalyst for innovative solutions and exemplar designs that can respond to the diverse objectives of our clients.

Stephen R. Hodder MBE
President, RIBA

About the author

Dale Sinclair is an architect and director of Dyer. As well as leading project teams on various award-winning projects, Dale is the author of *Leading the Team: An Architect's Guide to Design Management*. He is RIBA Vice President, Practice and Profession, an RIBA Board Member and Councillor and chair of the RIBA Large Practice Group. He also led the RIBA task group responsible for developing the landmark RIBA Plan of Work 2013 and authored the supporting publications, including the *Guide to Using the RIBA Plan of Work 2013*, as well as presenting several high-profile launch events across the UK.

Prior to this, he developed the *BIM Overlay to the RIBA Outline Plan of Work 2007*.

These projects have involved close collaboration with industry. Dale is also a member of the CIC BIM group and is on the management board of BuildingSMART UK.

Contents

Introduction

Assembling a Collaborative Project Team has been developed in conjunction with the RIBA Plan of Work 2013, the Overview publication (both available to download at www.ribaplanofwork.com) and the *Guide to Using the RIBA Plan of Work 2013*. It aligns with and supports these two landmark documents, providing more detailed guidance, specific activities and the focused tools that are essential for those responsible for and involved in assembling a project team. In particular, it considers how to create a truly collaborative project team and how achieving this during Stage 1 will make a project easier to run during the design, construction and operational stages. The guidance and tools can be referenced by any party involved at any stage of a project, but they are of greatest interest to the project lead and the lead designer. The RIBA Plan of Work 2013 can be used in isolation and the steps and tools outlined in this publication are not obligatory. However, even on simpler projects, the processes that are set out in the Plan can provide an invaluable resource for explaining to a client the proposed structure of the project team and a means of properly engaging each party in the project team. In the long run, their use will lead to clearer, more successful methods of working.

On paper, assembling a collaborative project team should be straightforward. In reality it is complicated due to:

- the number of parties that have to be appointed

- the various options for appointing each party

- variations in the timing of contractor involvement

- the different ways in which roles can be combined

- apportioning contractor and subcontractor design

- cultural issues associated with working together for the first time

- the parties' varying levels of experience gained on previous projects

- the lack of standard Schedules of Services for members of the project team, and

- the absence of common protocols and standards.

The steps and tools detailed in this publication reconcile these complexities by setting out a process that incrementally builds the collaborative project team, concluding with a number of documents that can work independently or as appendices to professional services contracts and the Building Contract.

It is essential for any collaborative project team to be constructed during Stage 0 (**Strategic Definition**) and Stage 1 (**Preparation and Brief**). The reasoning behind this requirement and the importance of these initial stages is considered in Chapter 1. By properly establishing the project team early in the project:

- design work can be undertaken without any ambiguities regarding responsibility

- clients can be certain that they have made sufficient allowances for fees and the design team members can be confident that their fees relate to detailed Schedules of Services

- clients can proceed, confident that the means of engaging the design team and the contractor have been fully considered, and

- every party is clear about their responsibilities and the information that they will deliver at each stage.

The RIBA Plan of Work 2013 considers the tasks undertaken by the project team rather than just those that are the responsibility of the design team. To fully understand the implications of this shift it is essential to consider the generic types of project team and to also understand how the different entities within project teams (the client, the design team and the contractor) have changed over the years. Chapter 2 considers the implications of these changes and looks at the evolution of the project team, likely changes in the future and how these impact on assembling a project team.

'Kick-starting' a project has its own complexities and unique considerations and these are set out in Chapter 3.

Having considered the importance of the early stages, the impact of the project team, rather than the design team, and how to begin the process, Chapter 4 examines how to strategically assemble a collaborative project team and the benefits that this brings. Where a project team regularly works together, the processes set out have additional benefits. They can be utilised to generate a clear and robust set of documents that can be used and continually improved from one project bid to the next, demonstrating stringent design management techniques.

Before looking at specific tools for assembling the project team, Chapter 5 considers the importance of the project brief and how it influences the process of assembling a project team.

Chapters 6, 7, 8 and 9 set out the detailed tools required to assemble the collaborative project team. The processes set out in these chapters:

- have been developed for use on projects where the client may be undertaking their first, and only, building project or for use by clients who regularly carry out projects

- consider the stage at which the contractor becomes involved in the process, ensuring that the project team is constructed accordingly

- work for both large and small projects

- ensure that the supporting documents required as appendices for professional services contracts or Building Contracts are properly conceived, and

- facilitate the preparation of the processes and protocols required by a collaborative project team using BIM.

Chapter 10 looks at the most frequently used forms of professional services contracts and Building Contracts required to bind the project team together and to provide the legal mechanisms to deal with any issues that may arise.

Finally, the appendix presents Multidisciplinary Schedules of Services, derived from the tasks set out in the RIBA Plan of Work 2013. Each task has been allocated to particular project roles but can be adjusted if necessary. The multidisciplinary format reduces the possibility of gaps or overlaps in the services provided and ensures that every member of the project team is aware of the tasks to be undertaken by each party.

You can access all of the practical tools for assembling a project team described in this book online at www.ribaplanofwork.com/toolbox.

In this book, the stages of the RIBA Plan of Work 2013 are set in bold (e.g. Stage 0 **Strategic Definition**) and terms which are defined in the RIBA Plan of Work 2013 Glossary are set with initial capitals (e.g. Building Contract).

1

Chapter

The importance of Stages 0 and 1

Chapter overview

Stage 2 is the most crucial stage of any project: the Concept Design is prepared, presented and signed off by the client. Robust Stage 2 outputs are an essential requirement of any project because any changes after Stage 2 can be difficult and costly to implement (as illustrated in Figure 1.1 below). Ensuring that Stage 2, and in particular the assembly of the project team, is undertaken as productively and effectively as possible is therefore a core project requirement. This chapter considers how the successful implementation of Stages 0 and 1 is central to achieving this aim.

Some would advocate the commencement of Stage 2 immediately. Why wait? What purpose do the earlier stages serve? Let's design! Let's get on site as soon as possible! With this in mind, this chapter dwells on the importance of Stages 0 and 1 and the crucial purpose that they serve. The *Guide to Using the RIBA Plan of Work 2013* also sets out how the requirements of Stages 6 and 7 can influence the earlier stages and these stages must also be considered before design work can commence.

If the best possible start to Stage 2 is to be achieved, some of the initial hurdles to assembling the collaborative project team need to be thought through. These are considered in Chapter 4. This chapter focuses on the importance and aims of Stages 0 and 1 and how their efficient use can facilitate a more effective and productive Stage 2.

The implication of change

Beyond Stage 2, the amount of information produced increases exponentially. The more information that is produced, the greater the amount of information that has to be amended in the event of a change. Significant changes proposed at Stage 3 might require the work of all of the design team to be altered and further reviews and coordination exercises to be undertaken, making these changes costly and difficult to implement.

At Stage 4 further, and significant, design team costs will be incurred, as will the costs of design work carried out by the contractor's specialist subcontractors. When a project reaches site, at Stage 5, the cost of change ramps up even further as change impacts on the ordering of materials, off-site fabrication costs and, in the most onerous of scenarios, the need to alter work already constructed on site.

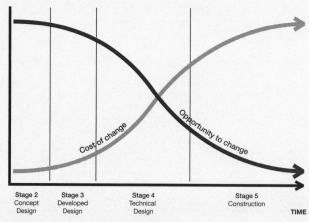

Figure 1.1 The cost of change

The impact of change: an example

By way of example, the following considers the implication of introducing an additional escalator into the ground floor of a shopping centre at different RIBA stages.

Stage 2 – Concept Design

The architect's information needs to be amended to include the escalator and the Cost Information has to be adjusted accordingly.

Stage 3 – Developed Design

The change is instructed via the project Change Control Procedures after a number of studies have been undertaken and the architect's information is amended followed by the structural and building services engineers' information. The Cost Information is also adjusted accordingly.

Stage 4 – Technical Design

Process as Stage 3; however, the architect must also alter the ground floor finishes and ceiling information and the balustrading setting out for level 1. The structural engineer must amend the substructure information as well as the detailed steelwork and slab information for level 1, and the building services engineer has to alter the electrical schematics and light fitting layout information on receipt of amended ceiling information from the architect. Depending on the timing, the specialist subcontractor providing the escalators would have to amend their information to show the additional escalator, the steelwork contractor would have to alter the secondary steelwork information and the contractor would have to consider any logistics issues arising from the changes. The lead designer would also be required to undertake additional coordination and integration exercises.

Stage 5 – Construction

Process as Stage 4; however, work already undertaken on site must be considered. Adjustment of the cast ground floor slab is required, secondary steelwork has not yet been delivered to site but requires modification and the ground floor tiling works have to be reprogrammed and the critical path reviewed.

Summary

This example demonstrates the additional work triggered by change and underlines the increased complexity at each stage. The cost of change will directly relate to the amount of activity undertaken, significantly increasing when fabricated or completed works on site have to be altered.

What is the aim of Stages 0 and 1?

In the extract from the RIBA Plan of Work 2013 in **Figure 1.2** below, the Core Objectives and Suggested Key Support Tasks of Stages 0 and 1 are set out. The rationale behind having two stages prior to the commencement of the **Concept Design** stage is straightforward: Stage 0 considers strategic issues and Stage 1 adds 'flesh' to these strategic bones. The outputs at the end of a successful Stage 1 would be:

- a robust **Initial Project Brief**, and

- a **collaborative project team**.

These two outputs and the connection between them are considered in detail below.

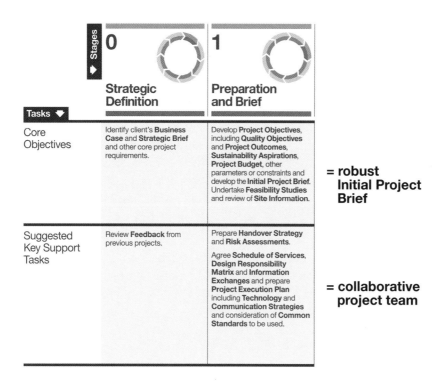

Figure 1.2 Extract from the RIBA Plan of Work 2013

Why a robust Initial Project Brief is crucial

Without a robust brief, the **Concept Design** stage cannot begin productively and, more crucially, may be taken in a direction that is not suited or aligned to a client's goals and objectives. It is fair to say that the brief needs to be developed in tandem with the developing Concept Design before it is finalised at the end of Stage 2, along with the Concept Design, but it is also essential to acknowledge that the brief and any associated Feasibility Studies should be sufficiently developed during Stage 1 to facilitate an effective start to Stage 2.

Stage 0

At Stage 0, the aim of the brief is to consider the client's Business Case and the strategic aspects of the project:

- Is the project, as anticipated by the client, taking the right strategic approach?

- What are the desired Project Outcomes?

- Is there a better way of achieving the desired outcomes?

- Is the site appropriate?

- Would refurbishment or an extension of an existing building be a more appropriate solution?

By stringently testing the client's Business Case and their initial thoughts on their requirements, all parties can proceed to Stage 1 confident that the Project Strategy is robust. This gives the client the comfort of knowing that the strategic aspects are correct and ensures that the project team is less likely to go down a 'blind alley' at Stage 1.

Stage 1

The goals of the briefing aspects at Stage 1 are to progress the client's detailed briefing requirements and to test them against the specific issues associated with the site as well as considering matters such as Project Outcomes, Sustainability Aspirations and the Project Budget. It is recognised that there is a fine line between briefing and feasibility aspects and the development of the Concept Design; however, a skilled 'briefmaker' will avoid making the leap to a design solution or drawing firm conclusions at this stage. In the *Guide to Using the RIBA Plan of Work 2013*, the increasing use of BIM 'briefing' models linked to an area schedule is noted as an example of how new briefing techniques and tools are facilitating more effective briefing processes.

The three briefing stages in the RIBA Plan of Work 2013 and their importance are considered further in Chapter 5.

What are the benefits of assembling the collaborative project team prior to Stage 2?

After strategically defining the project team at Stage 0, the assembly of the project team continues during Stage 1 until the majority of the team members, and certainly those undertaking the core project roles, have been appointed prior to Stage 2 commencing.

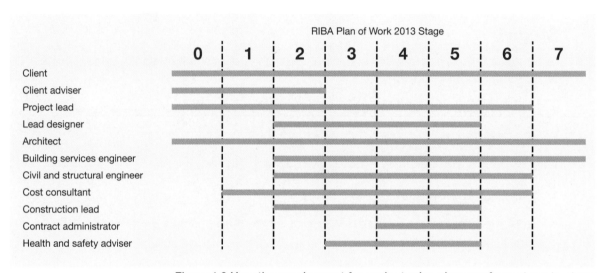

Figure 1.3 How the requirement for project roles changes from stage to stage

Figure 1.3 illustrates an example of which project roles might be required at each stage of a project, showing how the required roles vary from stage to stage with the number of project roles ramping up during the design stages and tapering back down following project handover at the end of Stage 6. If the additional project roles were to be considered, this tapering would be even more pronounced. This diagram underlines the need to properly conceive WHO will be in the project team at an early stage (as set out in Chapter 6). If this core strategic task is not carried out, the detailed tasks to be undertaken by each role (WHAT) cannot be prepared or adequate fee allowances made within the Cost Information.

There are a number of other important reasons for ensuring that the project team is properly assembled before Stage 2 commences:

- The shift from a design team to a project team results in the involvement of a greater number of parties, with a corresponding increase in the number of relationships that have to be managed and the creation, in turn, of a greater number of contractual relationships. Determining the interrelationships between all the members of the project team is therefore an important first step.

- The core project roles can be undertaken by different parties (see page 58). It is important to consider this aspect before assembling the project team.

- The additional project roles must be carefully considered to ensure that there are no overlaps or gaps in the work being undertaken by the core project team members and, more importantly, that the need and justification for the additional roles are clear to the client.

- The relationship between the project lead and the lead designer is crucial. The chemistry between these parties has to be perfect if the design stages are to be productive and respond positively to the client's goals and desired outcomes.

- The decision-making process has to be clarified. With the large number of project team members it is vital to be clear about who decides what and when?

- The timing of the contractor's involvement can vary. Determining this timing and how the contractor's role dovetails with those of the project lead and design lead is therefore of paramount importance and fundamentally dictates the procurement route.

- Specialist subcontractors can provide invaluable input and value engineering contributions to the design process and the timing and extent of their involvement is a crucial part of determining when the contractor comes on board. This input may be informal at Stage 3 or facilitated by overlapping Stage 3 and Stage 4 activities.

- Digital design technologies allow more complex design solutions to be developed quickly. Determining the nature of the project team early in the process ensures that each member of the team is not only aware of their design responsibilities and the level of detail to be produced at each stage but is also well versed in the protocols, procedures and other processes that are essential to the creation of an effective collaborative team.

Many clients who undertake multiple projects will have predefined ways of assembling their project teams and, of course, developing a team for a smaller project should be more straightforward. However, while both of these scenarios are more likely to be applicable to the practice approach described in Chapter 3, the tools set out later in this book can still provide an invaluable means of producing the documents used to appoint project teams time and time again.

What is the relationship between the brief and the collaborative project team?

A further complication deriving from the RIBA Plan of Work 2013 is that certain briefing issues require particular tasks to be included in Schedules of Services, and potentially the Building Contract, if they are to be successfully addressed. The following points should be considered:

- Setting Project Outcomes is part of the briefing process; however, if these outcomes are to be meaningful they will have to be measured post occupancy. New skills will be required to properly set the outcomes and to obtain accurate measurements. This will require the necessary Schedule of Services and contractual requirements to be included in the professional services agreements and the Building Contract.

- The preparation of design information traditionally ends with construction. With completed construction information now being used for the operation of buildings, it is necessary to consider at the early stages what information will be required post occupancy in order to operate the building. The information requirements must be included in the brief and the requisite contracts.

- While Stages 6 and 7 are geared to post-occupancy and in-use tasks, it is crucial to remember that information harvested during these stages will be used to inform future projects. It is important, therefore, to remember that Stages 6 and 7 will increasingly influence how a building is appraised, with Feedback and benchmarking informing a new project brief as the circle is completed and a new Stage 0 commences.

From the above points it can be seen that briefing and project team issues benefit from being considered in parallel, allowing the best possible project team for delivering the client's aspirations to be assembled for the commencement of Stage 2. There are further issues associated with the initial appointments which are considered in Chapter 3.

Summary

Many aspects have to be considered strategically at Stage 0 and in detail at Stage 1. Failure to properly consider these items may not impact directly on the design process but, if it does, it is likely that the impact will be significant. Conversely, if Stages 0 and 1 are properly harnessed, design can be efficiently carried out by the collaborative project team during Stage 2 and the chances of the Stage 2 outputs meeting or exceeding the client's expectations are greatly increased. Furthermore, by considering the brief and the project team in tandem, the right team will be created with the assembled collaborative project team more likely to deliver the client's objectives.

Chapter

The evolution of the project team

What is a project team?

Before considering how to assemble a project team it is essential to consider how the dynamics of the project team have changed over the years. A project team at its simplest level comprises those entities illustrated in **Figure 2.1**.

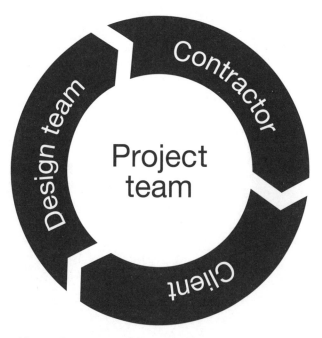

Figure 2.1 The entities and structure of the project team

This basic concept of a project team is still valid; however, cultural changes, such as the early involvement of the contractor, better informed clients, the increased scope of the design team and the range of procurement options available (including design and build, traditional, management contracting and other new ways of determining cost and allocating risk) create challenges in determining the best means of connecting the three entities of client, design team and contractor and have also altered the dynamics within each entity. There are many factors that now influence how a project team might be assembled and there is no longer a 'standard' approach.

Defining traditional and contractor-led project teams

New procurement routes have brought about significant changes in the mechanisms used by clients to enter into Building Contracts with contractors. While these may not have fundamentally altered the way that design work is carried out, they have dramatically changed the means of allocating risks and determining costs. Despite the multitude of procurement options that are available, only two project team structures exist. As the Stage 1 outputs may be developed differently depending on how the project team is to be structured, one of the strategic tasks for a client during Stage 0 is to develop a clear understanding of the differences between these team structures. The two generic team structures are:

- *the traditional project team* – in which the client appoints a design team to produce a design and to develop it to a certain level of detail. A number of contractors tender for the project with the successful contractor building the project

- *the contractor-led project team* – this project team is led by the contractor with the design team forming part of the contractor's team. A number of contractors will bid for a project, based on a comprehensive brief, with the winning tender being decided on the basis of design, cost and other factors.

Certain forms of procurement use a traditional project team during the early project stages and then revert to a contractor-led team by replacing (or novating – see page 19) the contractor as the client once the design has been developed to a specified stage. Under this arrangement, the contractor becomes responsible for all aspects of the design, including the work originally undertaken by the design team for the client in the early stages. Some clients believe that this results in 'the best of both worlds' as it enables them to deal directly with the design team in the early stages yet allows them to transfer all of the design risk to the contractor.

It is perhaps fair to say that the purest forms of contractor-led teams involve the contractor before the **Concept Design** stage commences, with the purest traditional project team involving the contractor at the latest possible point during Stage 4. For example, in the latter scenario, the traditional project team would tender for a contractor on the basis of all of the design work being completed. In reality, contractor involvement will usually commence somewhere in between the two stages suggested by these two examples and the amount and type of information contained in the Building Contract will vary. Furthermore, on most Building Contracts the contractor is responsible for discrete aspects of the design (this subject is tackled in greater detail on page 69). In scenarios where a transition from a traditional project team to a contractor-led team occurs, it is likely that this will occur midway through the design process with the precise timing dependent on a number of factors, such as risk transfer, cost and programme certainty, and the level of design development that the client wishes to see in the Employer's Requirements.

The traditional project team

The traditional project team has evolved over the years. When the RIBA Plan of Work was first conceived, the following were commonplace:

- the client would appoint the individual members of the design team

- the architect would be the project lead, lead designer and contract administrator

- a design would be produced by the design team

- the design team was responsible for all aspects of the design

- the client retained the risk (in relation to both cost and programme) for the duration of the project

- bills of quantities would be produced and the project tendered

- the successful contractor would be appointed under a JCT form of Building Contract

- Practical Completion would signify the handover of the building to the client, and

- up to a year later the Building Contract would be concluded.

More precisely, there was a common way of working that was consistently used on the vast majority of projects. Each member of the team understood their role and what was expected. However, despite the common method of working, buildings were frequently delivered late and over budget, primarily due to the adversarial environment triggered by the 'them and us' attitude that prevailed between members of the design team and the contractor, fuelled by the practice of lowest cost tendering, which required contractors to break even or make a profit by focusing on the changes made to the tendered design.

This established way of working has altered over the years, primarily as a consequence of changing procurement routes designed to resolve cost and programme issues but also in response to the increase in the amount of design work undertaken by specialist subcontractors appointed by the contractor.

On smaller projects, the design team is likely to consist of two or three parties, who are likely to have worked together before and have established effective, albeit informal, working processes. On larger projects, the design team is likely to comprise many parties and there is a strong likelihood that members of the team will be working together for the first time. This dynamic, different procurement routes, the increase of specialist subcontractor design and the increasing diversity of software and communication tools will inevitably result in different processes being adopted from project to project.

These variables can have a significant impact on a practice's processes and the risks can only be overcome if everyone agrees to adopt Common Standards and use 'plug and play' processes (see page 97).

Figure 2.2 The relationships in a traditional project team

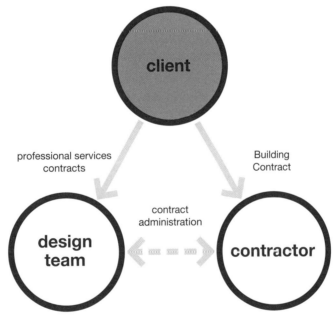

Why has the traditional project team changed?

Time, cost and quality are the three procurement mantras. Of these three, cost has been the biggest driver of change in the constitution of the project team, although time has also had a significant influence.

The effect of cost

Determining and fixing the cost of a project continues to remain the most challenging aspect of any project. Most clients are likely to have a fixed Project Budget. Traditional forms of tendering commonly use a 'contingency fund' to help to ensure that the building is delivered on budget but, even with this allowance, this result cannot be guaranteed. Design and build forms of contract will deliver cost and programme certainty; however, residual design and specification decisions that affect the quality of the finished building may be made by the contractor without reference to the client.

Traditional and one-stage design and build tenders may be returned over budget, requiring 'value engineering' to be undertaken in order to fine tune the design to fit the client's available Project Budget. This takes time and may compromise the initial design solution. By involving the contractor earlier, the contractor's supply chain can be involved in the design process at an earlier stage, unlocking innovation before the design progresses too far and certain design decision are 'fixed' or too difficult to change. However, two-stage design and build forms of procurement are statistically more expensive per square metre than one-stage forms, and contractor-led procurement means that the client is one step removed from the designers from the outset.

These examples underline the fact that both traditional projects and contractor-led projects, provided they are well managed, can result in the right outcomes for clients. A client therefore needs to consider the pros and cons of different procurement routes at the outset, along with the specific risks associated with the intended project, brief and site in order to select the most appropriate route in the circumstances.

The biggest challenge for any project team is devising a procurement strategy that will allow the design team and the contractor's designers (the specialist subcontractors) to engage earlier while allowing a fixed lump sum, or maximum cost, to be agreed between the client and the contractor before the design progresses too far.

The increased importance of specialist subcontractors

Regardless of the form of procurement used, specialist subcontractors now play a greater role in the design phases of a project. Contractor design work allows the skills of these designers to be harnessed by permitting the design team to design in a descriptive manner, enabling the specialist supply chain to unlock innovation or an individual specialist to propose a unique technical solution. Whether specialist subcontractors are used to drive down costs or to bring their unique technical capabilities to a project, the scope of their involvement must be clearly defined early on. This issue is covered in greater detail on page 69 where the purpose of the Design Responsibility Matrix is considered.

The effect of time

Time influences projects in two ways. Management contracts can be used to minimise the overall duration for the design and construction of a project but they require significant overlaps between design, procurement and construction. While management contracting is still widely employed, it is typically used only where the programme is the crucial driver and the client is willing to accept the cost risks associated with the overlap of design and construction and proceeding to site when the design is still at an early stage of development and before the majority of the costs have been determined by tender.

Although design and build forms of procurement have predominately been utilised to deliver cost certainty, an important by-product is programme certainty since the contractor has limited contractual leeway to deliver late and is likely to suffer significant financial penalties in the event of a late handover.

The evolution of the traditional team

In recent years, the traditional team has developed in a number of ways in response to the issues outlined, although these alterations can be seen more as tweaks than fundamental changes.

The changing leadership roles

On the majority of smaller projects, the leadership roles continue to be amalgamated and undertaken by the architect. On other projects, the relationships between the project lead, lead designer and contract administrator roles have evolved further and the parties undertaking these roles are likely to vary. For example, on design and build projects the project manager and contract administrator roles will be closely linked and the lead designer role may be diluted, particularly if some of the design team members are not novated to the contractor.

The novated design team

Novation is another evolutionary development of the project team. When a design team is novated, their employer ceases to be the original client and the contractor takes responsibility for the design team and their work. This typically includes responsibility for the work undertaken while the design team was working for the client.

This shift from a traditional project team to a contractor-led team allows the client to harness the best aspects of the two generic project teams: the client can liaise with the design team in the early stages and shape the emerging design appropriately, yet can hand over the cost and programme risks to a contractor.

Two-stage design and build was devised to allow the contractor to become involved in the project earlier, enabling clearer understanding of the project risks and allowing the earlier involvement of the contractor's supply chain as part of this process. To respond to the contractual changes that make them responsible for all aspects of the design, contractors have had to develop methods of managing the design process as well as means of assessing the capability of the designers for whom they are taking responsibility.

Appointing the design team as a single entity

Design team members have traditionally been appointed individually by the client and, in the majority of scenarios, clients will want to continue this practice. However, in recent years there have been an increasing number of cases in which the lead designer has been expected to select the design team members and be accountable for their performance and payments. This gives the lead designer greater control over who is to form part of the design team and the processes that will be used by the assembled team as well as encouraging innovation from one project to the next. However, this arrangement also creates additional risks, including the need to prepare subconsultant documents that are back-to-back with the lead designer's appointment, enhanced personal indemnity insurance (PII) requirements and greater financial risk in the event that the client is unable to pay invoices.

Nevertheless, it can be argued that this scenario is preferable to an 'arranged marriage', where the lead designer is responsible for coordinating the work of a design team, yet has had no say over the composition of this team. Certain clients overcome this hurdle by appointing the lead designer and then involving them in the selection process to determine the other members of the design team.

The use of framework contractors

Appointing the design team as a single entity resolves certain issues; however, it still does not address the question of how to involve the specialist subcontractors that can add value to the design process at an earlier stage in that process. Some clients who undertake regular building projects are overcoming this by setting up frameworks with contractors. These frameworks encourage contractors to provide more 'up front' contributions from their supply chain, allowing the design to progress holistically before a Building Contract is entered into.

The contractor-led team

All forms of design and build contracts require a contractor-led team, even if the team is formed by novating the original design consultants (see **Figure 2.3**). In recent years, projects undertaken under the Private Finance Initiative (PFI) have represented the purest forms of contractor-led procurement, although such contracts were more complex as the special purpose vehicles (SPV) set up to bid for them typically comprised a funder(s), a contractor and a facilities management (FM) contractor. Aside from cost and programme benefits derived from design and build procurement, contractor-led procurement is considered by clients for a number of reasons:

- *Early specialist contractor involvement* – arguably the biggest advantage of contractor-led procurement is the opportunity for the contractor to involve their supply chain at an early stage. At Stage 2, strategic contributions from the specialist subcontractors, whose input may dictate or influence the design direction of a particular concept, can be invaluable. At Stage 3, having input from those specialist contractors making the greatest contribution to the design process, which might typically be curtain walling or mechanical services contractors, can allow value engineering and innovation to be delivered earlier in the design process as well as providing a more robust coordination process. Put another way, early contractor involvement can ensure that the Developed Design is based on sound technical input and is therefore more robust at the commencement of Stage 4. Of course, many design teams will regularly work with the same specialist subcontractors and may involve them in the early design stages regardless of the form of procurement.

- *Single point of responsibility* – with contractor-led procurement, the client has a single point of responsibility. In the event that any issues arise during the course of the design and construction, or more importantly post occupancy, the client would discuss these issues with the contractor who would then determine whether the issue was a result of the design or the construction and resolve it accordingly.

- *Risk* – procurement options that involve a transition from a traditional project team to a contractor-led project team create additional risk for the contractor. The contractor is expected to take responsibility not only for what the incumbent design team have designed but also for what they have not designed! Furthermore, the contractor may have no experience of working with members of the client's design team. With contractor-led procurement the contractor, typically via the design manager, is fully aware of the status of the developing design and is party to design decisions, allowing risks to be understood, considered in greater detail and, where possible, eliminated. Furthermore, the contractor can select the parties that will make up their team.

Figure 2.3 The relationships in a contractor-led project team

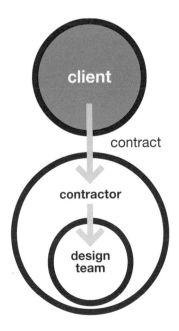

- *Operation and maintenance* – clients who are also end users are becoming more focused on the benefits of properly considering operational and maintenance issues during the early stages of the design and consider that contractors are best placed to ensure that such reviews are properly undertaken.

What are the downsides of a contractor-led solution?

The principal drawback of contractor-led project teams is the possibility that the level of design quality required or expected is not achieved. While most contractors involved in bidding for contractor-led forms of procurement understand that good design is required to win a tender, the client is one step removed from the design team and the design process. Ultimately, the client is selecting only the contractor and not the architect or the design team.

To overcome this perception, contractors will typically employ practices with design experience relevant to the particular sector or building type for which they are bidding and who are therefore most likely to deliver an innovative, and winning, concept. They will also utilise in-house design managers with a design background. However, in some circumstances the possibility exists that, following the award of a Building Contract, design decisions will be influenced or made by those with inappropriate design knowledge or training and clients must consider how this aspect will be dealt with under the terms of the Building Contract.

As with all forms of procurement, the client needs to consider how important design quality is and ensure that it is properly briefed as part of the Project Objectives, weighing this aspect against the importance of other elements, such as cost and programme certainty.

Collaborative working within project teams

In setting out the two generic project teams, no mention has yet been made of collaborative working or the collaborative contracts that are frequently cited as improving the efficiencies of the project team.

Assembling a Collaborative Project Team proposes that collaborative working methods primarily rely on 'soft' skills inherent in the individuals working in the project team. On the basis that the process for selecting the right parties and individuals focuses on this point, this book proposes that the best method of melding these individuals, and their practices and companies, into an effective project team is by ensuring that they are each fully aware of what they need to do and when they need to do it and by agreeing how they will work together.

The project team will still, however, need to use their soft skills to deliver the project effectively. These skills can be reinforced at the start of the project by undertaking team-building exercises or events as part of the workshop process for determining and agreeing the documents required, as detailed in this publication.

By determining who will do what, when and how, not only will a collaborative project team have been formed but, in the event that any issues arise and a dispute crystallises, there will be sufficient documentation to fall back on to ensure that the resolution of any such issues can be undertaken quickly and efficiently.

Collaborative contracts can assist the collaborative project team and the benefits of these are considered in Chapter 10.

More sophisticated collaborative teams can be formed by using 'gain/pain' mechanisms where all members of the project team share in the financial success, or failure, of a project. The level of pain in the event of a 'failure' may be capped and backed by an insurance policy. However, the essence is that with success incentivised, silo mentalities and blame cultures are less likely to occur. As the success of such projects is also based on soft skills or behaviours, they are not considered in detail within this publication, but such forms of working are entirely compatible with the tools presented in this book.

Finally, traditional and contractor-led project teams do not simply result in different procurement approaches. They give rise to different contractual approaches and fundamentally impact on the leadership of all aspects of a project, including design, cost and other elements. In order to develop a collaborative project team, the project leadership roles require careful consideration and the client must ensure that the parties appointed to undertake these roles understand and are aligned with the client's Project Objectives. For example, there is no point in having a project lead who is skilled in and focused on modular construction approaches if the client wishes a strong and unique design solution and, conversely, there is no point in considering a talented designer who does not value the contribution of the contractor, if the client wishes to unlock innovation across the whole project team.

The evolution of the project team entities

Having considered the evolution of the traditional project team and the development of contractor-led teams, it is important to consider how the three entities of the project team – the client, the design team and the contractor – have evolved before considering how to assemble a collaborative project team.

The more experienced and knowledgable client

Since the inception of the RIBA Plan of Work in 1963, the role and attitude of clients has changed in many ways. Those undertaking larger projects are usually more experienced and well versed in the processes involved in the design and construction of a building. On smaller projects, the proliferation of magazines and television programmes, particularly in relation to residential projects, has raised client expectations and some are well informed, very opinionated and may have their own ideas about what they want and how they might achieve their goals. Many clients of both types will select a practice on the basis of their published work, while others may source local architects based on discussions and fee proposals. Some will utilise the skills of a RIBA Client Adviser to help them navigate the early stages of a project successfully.

Experienced clients are likely to be sector-focused, and many sectors have client groups that meet to discuss current trends and issues specific to their own sector. By understanding issues across a number of projects, best practice in each sector can be distilled and more effectively applied. As a result, such clients expect their design team to have detailed sector knowledge and to be experienced in the delivery of the particular project type being commissioned.

Some clients directly employ a broad base of design and construction professionals who can bring additional insights to the design process and ensure that the work of the appointed design team is 'translated' in a manner that can be better understood within their own organisation.

Most crucially, clients are not always the end user. For example, the design team may be employed by a contractor or a developer and be remote from the end user. This creates communication issues as the design team can be one step, or several steps, removed from those who will occupy a building. This remoteness creates design and contractual challenges but, more significantly, it can make the achievement of the best Project Outcomes and right life cycle cost considerations more difficult to achieve.

Certain clients value design above cost and programme concerns. For example, a good design solution may be fundamental to their business or may be a core requirement for a residential client who will live in the completed project for a long time. However, some clients consider that design and build procurement can deliver appropriate design solutions as well as securing cost and programme certainty. Unfortunately, traditional procurement does not offer the time and cost advantages although, by carefully considering contingencies, properly preparing tender information and selecting the right contractor, these issues can be managed. Furthermore, new digital technologies (BIM), which result in more efficiently coordinated designs, might in turn lead to an increase in traditionally procured projects.

Some clients are focusing their attention on new subjects, such as Project Outcomes or operational and maintenance costs. Others are more interested in Feedback, Post-occupancy Evaluation or benchmarking that can be applied to future projects and methods of using the Project Information for the successful management of their building.

In conclusion, every client is different and each member of the project team must understand the objectives and goals of their particular client. The three-step briefing process (comprising the Strategic Brief, Initial Project Brief and the Final Project Brief) in the RIBA Plan of Work 2013 is designed to assist with this process.

The changing role of the contractor

The role of the contractor has changed. Previously, the rules of 'engagement' were better understood and a typical Building Contract was based on a substantial set of contract documents with the architect's instruction being the main tool for administrating the contract.

Design and build forms of contract have radically changed the contractor's approach. With risks passed over to them, contractors have had to develop risk management processes and achieve a clearer understanding of the Construction Programme and the critical path issues as well as the design process.

Contractors have become better at passing risks on to subcontractors and also at adjusting their own teams to reflect new ways of contracting. For example, a design manager is now a core role within any contractor team, regardless of the procurement route.

The increased role of the specialist subcontractor and the practice of harnessing their design abilities to bring innovation to the process started with the advent of management contracting. As design and build forms of contract emerged in the 1990s, this trend continued and enabled contractors to pass on design responsibilities to their supply chain. JCT Building Contracts accepted this form of working and contractor design work is now commonplace on the majority of traditional JCT projects.

The timing of the contractor's involvement can vary for a number of reasons and one of the core considerations of the RIBA Plan of Work 2013 has been aligning the contractor involvement inherent in different procurement routes to a particular stage. The benefits of early contractor engagement are that:

- specialist subcontractors can be involved and engaged earlier

- construction risks and buildability issues can be properly considered at the earliest possible stage

- site logistics issues can be better understood and developed, and

- more accurate Cost Information can be obtained.

The downside can be difficulties in agreeing an acceptable contract sum when the contractor believes that it is in a good negotiating position (research carried out by various cost consultants shows that two-stage design and build tenders result in higher costs per square metre) and a tendency for the exploration of detailed aspects of the design to distract from the development of a robust Concept Design.

In summary, contractor-led procurement is now well established and is becoming a common way of working, particularly on larger projects. The design processes used on such projects are likely to be very well developed. However, ways of understanding and agreeing the cost of a project and the allocation of risk still continue to develop and evolve.

The increased complexity of the design team

A design team typically comprises:

- the core designers: the architect and structural and building services engineers

- the project lead and lead designer

- the cost consultant

- additional consultants providing specialist advice

- health and safety advisers

- the Building Contract administrator, and

- consultants providing strategic advice, including client advisers.

The tasks undertaken by the design team have not changed fundamentally over the years, particularly in the early design stages; however, the following are now commonplace:

- More specialists (such as masterplanners, acoustic consultants and fire engineers) are typically involved. This requires additional design management time and effort to ensure that the contributions of these specialists are properly defined in line with the project requirements and coordinated with the work of other members of the design team.

- Certain aspects of the detailed design are undertaken by specialist subcontractors. This requires close attention from the lead designer, who must coordinate work undertaken by design team members as well as integrating the work of the specialist subcontractors into the coordinated design.

- Different methods are used to obtain tenders for projects from contractors. These can impact on and vary the cost interface between the client, the design team (including the cost consultant) and the contractor.

- The role of project lead is more complex as it must deal with the management of the project team and the broader project issues.

- Some project roles may be undertaken by different parties (for example, the architect, project lead, cost consultant or a standalone company may all be capable of performing the main health and safety role).

While these changes may not have altered the way in which design work is undertaken, the increased complexities and variability of the tasks and processes require more experienced leadership and a re-evaluation of the management roles.

The lead designer is a core role that has to be undertaken by one of the designers. This would typically be the architect, although on certain projects others may be better placed to fulfil this role (for example, the mechanical and electrical (M&E) designer on a process facility, such as a data centre).

How do these changing roles affect the project team?

It is likely that traditional project teams will exist for the foreseeable future and that such teams, along with contractor-led teams, will continue to evolve as clients attempt to balance design quality, programme and cost/risk aspects while working towards methods of guaranteeing better Project Outcomes.

The processes now involved in designing, constructing, maintaining and using a building are more complex and there is much more to consider. To say that things have moved on would be a huge understatement. The following aspects must now all be considered:

- the architect does not always lead the design team

- many clients have their own internal professional advisers

- more roles and more parties are involved in the process

- the design team may be employed in many different ways using various forms of professional services contract

- the timing of the contractor's involvement varies, depending on the procurement route used

- numerous options for Building Contracts exist

- the contractor and, by extension, specialist subcontractors are responsible for many aspects of the design

- the lead designer is increasingly responsible for coordinating the work of the design team and integrating the work of specialist subcontractors

- likewise, the allocation of cost and programme risk varies

- post-occupancy duties are more commonplace and, most crucially,

- new digital technologies are radically changing the way we work.

So, there are now many factors that influence how a project team might be assembled and there is no 'standard' approach. Chapter 3 considers how these variables complicate the 'kick-starting' process with Chapter 4 looking at the holistic nature of the collaborative project team before Chapters 6 to 9 set out the detailed tools required to assemble the collaborative project team.

What is driving further changes to the project team?

To complicate matters still more, a raft of new topics that impact on the design stages are being embraced by clients. Many of these, such as life cycle costs or Project Outcomes, are not new; they were just not addressed in the majority of projects or considered by a high percentage of clients. This situation is now changing. For example, sustainability has become a more important topic and clients now expect the many subjects that may be part of their Sustainability Aspirations to be embraced as part of 'standard' design processes.

Of course, the biggest driver for change is currently the new technologies that allow the data in the various information models to be harnessed for post-occupancy purposes, including facilities management. Contractors are also seeing the benefits of harnessing such technologies to drive out inefficiencies in the design process and to eliminate waste on site by ensuring that all design issues are resolved on computer and not on site. Greater use of modularisation and prefabrication is anticipated.

From the design team's perspective, more practices are employing specialists, such as:

- mathematicians and programmers to assist in the development and understanding of more complex geometries

- coding experts to ensure that information can be delivered in the appropriate format at project handover, and

- behavioural experts who can suggest ways of 'nudging' the behaviour of a building's occupants.

These new subjects, new technologies and new specialisms will result in both traditional and contractor-led project teams continuing to evolve and the dilemma of securing early contractor involvement within acceptable cost parameters will continue to encourage refinements to the project team designed to facilitate collaborative working and ways of unlocking innovation from all members of the project team.

Summary

Many aspects of the design process have changed and new duties are providing new challenges and opportunities. The practices which adapt to the enormity of these changes will be those setting the trends for the future of practice. Clients will continue to use either traditional or contractor-led project teams and both types of team therefore need to be understood. While the use of contractor-led teams (particularly those using the novation of a traditional project team) is on the increase, better coordination processes and collaborative working techniques might result in a resurgence of traditional project teams.

3

Chapter

Achieving the best
possible start to a project

The 'kick-starting' process (the practice or project approach)

The practice approach

The project approach

Chapter overview

Chapter 1 set out the reasons why the early project stages are crucial. Chapter 2 considered the generic types of project team and how these might impact on a project. Before considering how to assemble a collaborative project team (Chapter 4) in response to the observations made in the earlier chapters, this chapter considers the importance of the 'kick-starting' process and the means of selecting the initial members of the project team. This process is crucial as these initial parties will be responsible for assembling the collaborative project team and ensuring that the best possible brief is put in place.

The commencement of a project is crucial because the decisions made by the client at that point in time, and resultant initial appointments that are made, have a fundamental impact on how the project team will subsequently be assembled. The initial appointments are also likely to influence who will prepare the Concept Design, the quality of the design that is produced and how project and design management issues, and therefore risk, will be dealt with, as well as determining how the three procurement mantras of time, cost and quality will be considered, presented to the client and agreed.

In other words, the initial appointments required to 'kick-start' the RIBA Plan of Work process are crucial decisions.

The 'kick-starting' process (the practice or project approach)

While the type of project and its size and complexity will have a degree of influence on the initial appointments, it is more likely that the decisions will be driven by the client's experience, knowledge and expectations. These, and the initial connections to members of the project team, are likely to vary significantly. For example, one residential client may have read many design magazines, watched a number of TV programmes and may be well versed in the subject, having the confidence to approach a number of architects whose work they admire. Another may have had no specific aspirations to commission a project and have been convinced to extend a property following a casual meeting at a social event.

Regardless of the extent of a client's experience, those undertaking a project for the first time will rely on, and trust, the early advice they receive. Whether a new school, university, hospital or house is proposed, the project team appointed at the early stages will shape the client's views and opinions, no matter how objective they attempt to be. These early decisions are therefore extremely important.

Experienced clients are more familiar with the 'kick-starting' process and, therefore, making the initial appointments will be more straightforward.

For simplicity's sake, this publication considers two scenarios: a 'practice' approach and a 'project' approach. The detail of these approaches is set out below and is similar to the concept of the bespoke practice- or project-specific RIBA Plan of Work 2013.

Neither approach impacts on how the incremental development of the project brief should be carried out; however, as the brief is a core tool at Stage 2, and because some of its contents may require specific services to be included in the professional services contracts or the Building Contract, it is considered in **Figures 3.1** and **3.2**. The complexity of both preparing the project brief and assembling the project team is likely to increase with the size and/or complexity of a project, but the processes set out in this publication provide benefits on even the smallest of projects as they bring greater clarity to who is doing what, when they are doing it and how the project team will work together collaboratively.

The practice approach

Use of the practice approach is anticipated in two sets of circumstances:

- for experienced clients who understand the processes involved and have their own in-house appointment documents prepared for use on every project

- for architectural practices, or project managers and others, where a common set of documents can be prepared for use on all of the practice's projects, although the clients themselves will vary from project to project and also vary in their level of experience.

The practice approach of assembling the project team uses the same tools as the project approach. The difference is that the tools are progressed 'off-line' (i.e. not in relation to a specific project). The concept is straightforward: the WHO, WHAT, WHEN and HOW aspects (see Chapters 6 to 9) are considered holistically and then utilised on every project. The WHY aspects are part of the briefing process and need to be considered individually on each new project.

The practice approach is summarised in **Figure 3.1**.

The step change is that, while the project approach relies on strategic considerations and appointments during Stage 0 and the detailed assembly of the project team during Stage 1, the practice approach works on the basis that each member of the project team is appointed at the outset, for the duration of the project, on the basis of fully developed appointment documents. There is therefore no incremental development of the project team.

The practice approach can be harnessed by an architectural practice, an experienced client or a project manager undertaking the project lead role, and the tools in this publication can be used by any party. The fundamental difference is that the party that has their foot in the door and is appointed at the outset

Figure 3.1 The practice approach

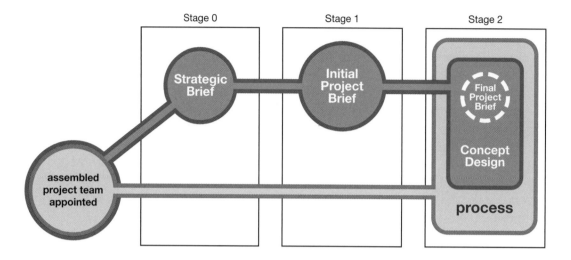

takes responsibility for ensuring that the client is aware of how the entire project team is to be assembled and, more importantly, takes responsibility for ensuring that all of the necessary design team and contractor appointments are properly made (for example, without any gaps in Schedules of Services or other documents required to contractually assemble the project team).

For those considering this approach, it is possible to skip the next section and go straight to Chapter 4.

The project approach

The project approach is more appropriate for larger or complex projects that might benefit from a stringent review of the client's requirements and a more thorough assessment of the type of project team that is required. The project team structure is likely to be more complex and the issues of time, quality and cost will have greater implications and require strategic consideration. The project approach can be used by:

- an inexperienced client, to help steer them through the early project stages of any project

- experienced clients on projects where the project team selection needs to be more rigorous and where a practice approach may not be relevant, or

- the project lead, to ensure that the project team selection process is robust based on, and in response to, project-specific drivers.

Where the project approach is harnessed by inexperienced clients, the initial appointments are crucial as the party commissioned to undertake Stage 0 has to assist the client with significant strategic decisions. RIBA Client Advisers can perform this crucial role and provide the strategic advice necessary prior to longer term appointments being made.

An experienced client may harness the project approach in conjunction with the practice approach. This hybrid approach is undertaken by preparing certain documents on a practice basis with others generated or adjusted to deal with the unique aspects of a specific project.

While the tools in Chapters 6 to 9 can be used in isolation, they might be developed in a workshop environment during Stages 0 and 1. This approach can be an effective way of ensuring that the client's priorities are properly considered and of making certain that the reasoning behind core project team decisions is aligned with the client's goals for design quality, cost and programme.

Figure 3.2 shows how the project approach works and how the two parallel strands of developing the project brief and assembling the project team relate to each other, with the project brief and project team both progressed incrementally prior to Stage 2 commencing.

With the project approach, further commissions may be required prior to Stage 1 commencing or to assist with the development of the project brief or assembling the project team. The decision of whether to assemble a traditional or a contractor-led team may also influence who is appointed at Stage 1.

In either case, at the start of Stage 1 the backbone of the project team should have been established and commissioned to focus on preparing the Initial Project Brief and assembling the project team for the commencement of the Concept Design at Stage 2.

Figure 3.2 The project approach

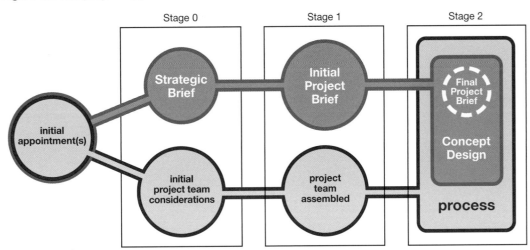

34

Summary

Depending on the experience of the client and the nature and complexity of a project, a practice or project approach, or a mixture of both, may be appropriate. The client must take into account the fact that the initial appointments are likely to be influential in determining the culture of the assembled project team and the advice that is provided, and that these initial appointments therefore need to be carefully considered. The tools set out later in the book are appropriate for either approach.

Chapter

Assembling the collaborative project team

Why is a collaborative project team required?

The WHY, WHO, WHAT, WHEN and HOW of a project

The collaborative issue of the WHAT and HOW documents

Why is a collaborative project team required?

Chapter 2 mentioned the 'them and us' attitude that has historically existed in the construction industry. The only way of breaking through this cultural barrier is to harness collaborative project teams where all members of the team work together to achieve the client's goals and objectives. Until the culture of our industry has changed this will, of course, be a significant challenge, particularly when the intuitive skills and interests of each member of the team may be in conflict. For example, the architect may have created a Concept Design that meets the client's objectives and is aligned to the difficulties of a historic site but the contractor may judge the design to be complex to construct and may consider a simpler design solution more appropriate. This is, of course, an extreme example; however, it highlights how quality, cost and time variables need to be considered by the client and their resolution assigned to those best placed to manage them. It also flags up the biggest conundrum in the construction industry: the interface between the design team and the contractor and how to make this core relationship work more effectively.

To achieve effective collaboration, the client may select a procurement route that harnesses early contractor engagement but this step in itself may not resolve all the issues of the interface. For this core interface to be effective:

- the design team needs to consider construction and buildability issues as the design progresses and respect and respond to the difficulties that may be encountered on site

- the contractor has to understand the rationale behind the design concept and respect the reasoning behind a particular approach

- ways of communicating the project risks must be agreed so that they can be understood and managed by the most appropriate member of the project team

- means of progressing the Cost Information for the developing design and, more importantly, the means of transferring the cost risk from the design team to the contractor have to be considered, and

- methods of harnessing the design skills of the specialist subcontractors, and potential value engineering items that may result from the early interface between the design team and the contractor's supply chain, have to be developed.

Of course, this highlights only one set of relationships. Many others exist: between design team members, between the cost consultant and the design team, and so on. Chapter 2 highlighted the differences between working collaboratively and assembling a collaborative project team and it is true that a major contribution to a collaborative project team is ensuring that each team member is a good communicator, is open to the ideas of others and respects the inputs from, and skills of, all members of the team.

This publication does not consider how individuals obtain these skills. However, there is another fundamental way of considering the collaborative project team. *Assembling a Collaborative Project Team* advocates that by stringently developing and agreeing the WHY, WHO, WHAT, WHEN and HOW aspects of a project during Stages 0 and 1, the resultant project team will:

- work together more effectively

- be able to commence the Concept Design stage with a robust brief in place

- encounter no ambiguities in relation to design responsibilities, and

- have documents in place for reference in the event of a dispute.

The WHY, WHO, WHAT, WHEN and HOW of a project

WHY — **WHY** relates to the brief and the client aspects; for example, **WHY** do we need a new building?

WHO — **WHO** considers the roles required on a project at each project stage and then allocates the roles to generic organisations before specific companies are appointed. The **WHO** process is strategic in its nature.

WHAT — **WHAT** examines the tasks that each party needs to undertake at each stage of the project, design responsibilities and the information that will be exchanged at the end of each stage? The **WHAT** aspects are a core contractual requirement for every party in the project team and represent the practical detail of assembling the project team. By considering **WHAT** in detail, the potential for ambiguities when the project team members are working together is significantly reduced.

WHEN — **WHEN** advocates a strategic programme that sets out the key project milestones to be added to the relevant contracts and incorporated into more detailed design and Construction Programmes.

HOW — **HOW** considers the means that the various parties will use to work together, the technologies they will employ and the methods of communication, including the exchange of information. In essence, **HOW** the day-to-day running of the project will be undertaken. **HOW** encourages the use of Common Standards to make the design process as streamlined as possible.

This book advocates assembling the project team using the following process to determine the WHY, WHO, WHAT, WHEN and HOW aspects:

- The WHY aspects are considered with the client (see Chapter 5).

- The WHO and WHEN aspects are developed by the project lead, possibly in conjunction with the lead designer. These set the scene for preparing the WHAT documents.

- The WHAT aspects are developed by the project lead and the lead designer to allow fee proposals by all parties to be prepared and submitted.

- The HOW aspects are prepared for discussion by all members of the project team. Some clients may have prescriptive requirements whereas in other cases the project team may develop the Project Execution Plan.

- The WHY, WHO, WHAT, WHEN and HOW are bound as required into the professional services contracts and operational or Building Contracts.

- The WHY, WHO, WHAT, WHEN and HOW outputs continue to be used for the duration of the project to ensure that the day-to-day management of the project is successful.

The completed documents, bound into the contractual documents, also provide supporting evidence in the event of a dispute; however, the holistic nature of the preparation is aimed at avoiding any disputes arising in the first place. This might be defined as the 'contractual non-contractual' approach.

Figure 4.1 The relationship between assembling the collaborative project team tools and professional services contracts and operational or Building Contracts

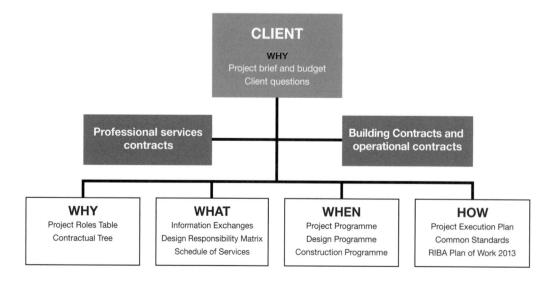

Figure 4.1 illustrates this concept. Of greatest importance is the fact that the outputs (detailed in **Figure 4.2**) are all concluded prior to design work commencing in earnest at Stage 2. The significance of the WHY aspects becomes clearer in Chapter 5, and the rationale behind the WHO, WHAT, WHEN and HOW aspects, and the more detailed tools that are used to produce the necessary outputs, are set out in Chapters 6 to 9.

Figure 4.2 The outputs in the RIBA Plan of Work 2013 in relation to WHY, WHO, WHAT, WHEN and HOW

Strategic Brief and Initial Project Brief **Project Budget**	**WHY**
Project Roles Table **Contractual Tree**	**WHO**
Schedules of Services **Design Responsibility Matrix** **Information Exchanges**	**WHAT**
Project, Design and Construction **Programmes**	**WHEN**
Project Execution Plan including Technology and Communications Strategies	**HOW**

Regardless of whether a project team is to be assembled in a practice or project manner or whether it is a traditional or contractor-led project team, *Assembling a Collaborative Project Team* advocates the preparation of a number of documents that consider the WHO, WHAT, WHEN and HOW aspects of a project in parallel with and/or in response to the WHY aspects, covered in the next chapter.

The outputs resulting from the above process of considering the WHY, WHO, WHAT, WHEN and HOW aspects are summarised in **Figure 4.2**. They are all embedded into the RIBA Plan of Work 2013.

Devising the Project Roles Table and the Contractual Tree (WHO) and the Project Programme (WHEN) are relatively straightforward activities. However, the WHAT and HOW aspects create bigger challenges and will take longer to produce. The WHAT and HOW documents may be influenced by the development of the brief and they may impact on the design process. They should, ideally, be prepared by a party with a design background or sufficient experience of allocating design responsibility and preparing detailed schedules of services for design team members. The lead designer, who will have responsibility for coordinating the work and integrating the designs of other project team members, might prepare the initial versions of certain documents although the project lead may also have the experience to undertake this task. The project lead will certainly have a degree of input to ensure that any management or other tasks required to successfully deliver the project, or to make certain that tasks which are required to deliver post-occupancy outcomes, are properly set out and included in the detailed Schedule of Services.

The collaborative issue of the WHAT and HOW documents

In the following chapters, the tools for determining the WHY, WHO, WHAT, WHEN and HOW aspects are set out. As noted above, the HOW and WHEN aspects are the more straightforward documents to produce. These outputs may need to be updated during Stage 1 as the structure of the team develops since, in the initial stages, before any contracts are concluded, there are no major strategic issues to be considered in relation to them.

The WHAT and HOW aspects create one issue in relation to the collaborative team: if the project team is to be truly collaborative, each party in the team should agree and be comfortable with the specific aspects of the WHAT and HOW documents that will impact on their services.

However, to properly obtain fee quotations for these services, the project lead, with the assistance of the lead designer, will have to prepare initial versions of these documents. It is therefore essential to ensure that each party is given adequate opportunity to comment on the suite of documents at tender stage to allow any refinements to be made. However, it must be remembered that if the services of one party are adjusted, the relevant services need to be added or deleted from another party's Schedule of Services and the Design Responsibility Matrix incorporating Information Exchanges reconsidered.

Ultimately, the aim is to ensure that the documents for all members of the project team have been agreed and, more importantly, that they interrelate and dovetail with each other. It is for this reason that the majority of the tools in *Assembling a Collaborative Project Team* are multi-party, ensuring that the risk of gaps or overlaps in who will do WHAT and HOW is minimised.

Chapter 5 examines the documents that relate directly to the client (WHY), with Chapters 6 to 9 addressing the WHO, WHAT, WHEN and HOW aspects required to establish the collaborative team. Chapter 10 considers how these can be used in conjunction with the range of professional services contracts and operational or Building Contracts that exists to contractually bind the project team together.

Summary

Assembling a Collaborative Project Team encourages the use of tools that allow the project team to be assembled incrementally (WHO), defining the specific obligations of each party and the information that they will deliver at each stage (WHAT), as well as determining the various Project Programmes (WHEN) and the protocols and procedures (HOW) that everyone will follow. The completed documents can be utilised as appendices for inclusion in the relevant contracts and, more importantly, they become tools that can be used in the day-to-day running of a project.

Chapter

The relationship between the project brief and the collaborative team

The brief as the WHY component

The three stages of the project brief

The Project Budget

The stage outputs (or Information Exchanges)

Chapter overview

The briefing process is a core interface between the client and the project team and a successful briefing process is essential if the assembled collaborative team is to be effective at Stage 2 and, more importantly, if the Project Outcomes are to be achieved at project handover. This chapter considers strategic briefing issues and how the briefing process relates to the assembly of the project team.

The Concept Design will be prepared in response to the contents of the Initial Project Brief. In addition to the information necessary to facilitate the design stages, some clients, particularly those who are more experienced, might include other aspects in the brief. For example, the information to be exchanged at each stage (see page 72) or the Communication Strategy or other protocols that they may require the design team and the contractor to follow. The brief might also stipulate specific information that the client requires at project handover for the running of the building. On this basis, the brief might comprise:

- the strategic requirements of the project

- the functional requirements of the project

- the desired Project Outcomes

- the Project Objectives including Quality Objectives

- the project's Sustainability Aspirations, and

- the Project Budget (see page 45).

This chapter is not intended to provide comprehensive advice on briefing; however, the project brief is an essential client document and its purpose needs to be clearly understood if the right professional services contracts are to be prepared. It develops incrementally: strategically at Stage 0, in detail at Stage 1 and fine-tuned in response to the Concept Design proposals (see below) at Stage 2. It also relates to the assembling of the project team as Schedules of Services may be required to ensure that the requirements of the brief are met. As the brief develops, some aspects of it may be superseded by the WHO, WHAT, WHEN and HOW outputs.

In some instances the brief will be contractual. This is more likely to be the case for contractor-led forms of procurement where the brief may act as the Employer's Requirements forming part of a tender process. In these situations, the order of precedence between the brief and the developing design and the Contractor's Proposals needs careful consideration. For example, a comprehensive brief might include subjective design aspects (such as 'design a secure environment' or 'public spaces to be bright and airy') as well as prescriptive items (such as 'staff common rooms to have a minimum of eight sockets'). In this example, when the Building Contract is signed, some aspects of the brief will be superseded by the Contractor's Proposals and the subjective items may need to be deleted from the brief with the prescriptive items retained in the version included in the Building Contract.

The brief as the WHY component

For simplicity and clarity, *Assembling a Collaborative Project Team* considers the brief as the WHY component. The reasoning behind this is that the briefing process summarises and concludes all of the discussions with the client. For example:

- Why is a new building required?

- Why is only a particular part of the site being considered?

- Why is a traditional project team preferred?

- Why is a three-year period from commencement to project handover crucial?

- Why are fortnightly meetings proposed?

Who should prepare the brief?

An important initial consideration is deciding WHO should prepare the project brief. Professional clients may have the in-house capability or may use external advisers to assist them in the process. The brief that they prepare is also likely to be more detailed and require longer to develop. There are advantages in using an architect, perhaps a RIBA Client Adviser, to prepare the brief. This would allow initial Feasibility Studies to be prepared in parallel to test the robustness of the brief. This adviser might also be retained to comment on design proposals prepared by the appointed architect as part of a traditional or contractor-led project team.

Depending on the circumstances, and certainly on smaller projects, it makes sense for the brief to be prepared by the architect who is also appointed to develop the design proposals. In many situations this is sensible, as there is a fine line between the design work required to carry out the Feasibility Studies necessary to ratify the Initial Project Brief and the emergence of a Concept Design. Moreover, the briefing process and the close liaison with the client inevitably results in a good understanding of the project, acting as a natural springboard to the Concept Design stage. Architects joining the project team at Stage 2 may query strategic matters or require clarification of certain decisions before they are confident that the brief is robust. There will inevitably be a learning curve. These are further conundrums for the client to consider.

The remainder of this chapter considers the following client issues:

- the project brief bridges the first three stages of the RIBA Plan of Work 2013 – the reasoning behind this arrangement is set out below

- the Project Budget, which is crucial as it has a fundamental relationship with the Concept Design proposals

- the information exchanged at each stage, which can vary depending on numerous factors, including the client's requirements and the questions that they may need answered at a given stage.

The brief is used to capture client discussions and positively concludes the WHY questions, allowing the project team to move forward confidently. However, it may also impact on the WHO, WHAT, WHEN and HOW aspects required to deliver the Project Objectives, and therefore the brief and its relationship to other documents (many of which will be contractual in nature) need careful consideration.

The three stages of the project brief

The project brief is a core project document during the initial project stages. The RIBA Plan of Work 2013 envisages three stages of brief development with the Final Project Brief being agreed at the end of Stage 2 in parallel with the client's agreement to the Concept Design. This does not mean that the brief is necessarily 'frozen'. It underlines the fact that change following the commencement of Stage 3 can have significant cost implications (as outlined on page 6) and therefore proposed changes to the brief, or indeed any change, should be dealt with using a stringent change control process. The purposes of the three briefing stages are outlined below.

Strategic Brief at Stage 0

The purpose of the Strategic Brief is straightforward: it should address the client's Business Case and Core Objectives. For example, is a new building required? Would an alternative approach achieve the desired outcomes? Should an existing building be extended or refurbished? Where a number of sites are considered, which meets the strategic goals of the client best?

Initial Project Brief at Stage 1

The Initial Project Brief should begin to put more flesh onto the bones of the Strategic Brief. It should consider specific spatial requirements, the desired Project Outcomes, Sustainability Aspirations, Quality Objectives and the Project Budget (see below). Depending on the nature of the project, it may contain very precise and detailed information that may be contractual (for example, room data sheets with environmental and other building services parameters).

Feasibility studies might be required to test the relationship between the site and the core brief requirements to make sure that the brief is as robust as possible prior to the commencement of the Concept Design stage.

The definition of Project Outcomes needs careful consideration, particularly if it is intended that they become contractual requirements that will be measurable on completion. When the client intends to use the information produced during the design stages for the operation of the building, this fact must be included in the brief to ensure that the developing design takes cognisance of any such requirements.

Final Project Brief at Stage 2

Finalising the brief at the end of Stage 2 acknowledges that the iterative design process may require changes to the brief. The Final Project Brief should be aligned with the Concept Design that is signed off by the client at the end of Stage 2.

While the brief may not change beyond the end of Stage 2, aside from items dealt with under the Change Control Procedure, as the level of detail contained in the Project Information progresses it may be necessary for members of the project team to ratify compliance with the project brief. This step requires careful consideration depending on the contractual status of the brief. For example, if the brief is contractual and takes precedence over the developing design information, issues may arise at a future date if a problem occurs and the completed building does not comply with the requirements of the Final Project Brief. This relationship must be carefully considered and understood by all members of the project team.

The Project Budget

Understanding the Project Budget is an essential requirement at Stage 1. At its simplest level, the Project Budget might comprise the funds available for the construction of the project as well as the associated fees from the design team. On more complex projects, the project lead, lead designer and cost consultant may have to consider:

- design fees

- enabling works, such as services installations

- pre-construction preliminary costs from the contractor

- costs from a number Building Contracts

- allowances for finishes, fittings and equipment, which may not be included in the main Building Contract

- removal and other move management costs

- maintenance during the initial occupation period

- and, occasionally, the operational costs for a period of time.

In simple terms, when developing the strategic project brief it is essential to understand the budget that the client has available and what they expect to achieve for these funds. A core function of Stage 0 is understanding these issues strategically. For example, if a client requires a new 2,000 m² college and the cost consultant advises that £1,500 per m² would be the typical cost for a building of this type, size and location, the Project Budget would have to include a £3,000,000 allowance for construction. If the proposed budget is less than this, the strategic aspects can be addressed before design work commences.

During Stage 2, an estimate for the construction cost will have to be prepared and included within the Cost Information submitted at the end of the stage for comparison with the Project Budget. Where the Cost Information exceeds the Project Budget, the design team will have to alter the Concept Design until it is affordable (remembering that this should have been strategically determined during Stage 0) or the client will need to agree to adjust the Project Budget.

In summary, the cost of the developing design proposals must be aligned to the client's budget until the point in time when the cost can be fixed and some or all of the cost risk transferred to the contractor via the Building Contract.

The process of costing a developing design is not straightforward; however, it has to be recognised that the production of cost estimates is part of the iterative design process and not a separate activity undertaken at the end of each stage. In developing Schedules of Services, the project lead, together with the lead designer and the cost consultant, must consider carefully how this will be achieved.

The stage outputs (or Information Exchanges)

One of the core themes of the RIBA Plan of Work 2013 is the inclusion of the Information Exchanges task bar. This task bar has been devised to acknowledge that the deliverables at each stage may vary, depending on the client's requirements and the circumstances related to each project. Furthermore, a client may only require the services to be undertaken up to a particular stage. One trend that was identified in the Plan of Work consultations was limited Schedules of Services being undertaken by some clients where the planning risk was high. This creates a number of issues. For example, the design may not be sufficiently robust when it is developed further following the granting of planning consent and may require further and difficult negotiations during the **Developed Design** stage.

During the detail design stage, different levels of detail may be required by different clients. For example, one residential client may require detailed drawings to ensure that joinery work is carried out to the highest possible standard whereas another may require only the bare minimum to allow the contractor to tender and for planning consent to be obtained.

These scenarios underline the fact that different client information requirements create different project risks and different resource requirements. Agreeing the project Information Exchanges is therefore a core project requirement in order to manage the risks associated with project- or client-specific issues.

Client questions at each stage

The UK Government is adding a further take on this subject by considering the questions that are required to be answered at each stage. Design teams customarily produce stage reports, typically based on a practice's standard way of working. The RIBA Plan of Work has never been prescriptive in this regard and no specific guidance exists, and as a result the content of such reports varies widely. The UK Government is less interested in what a design team typically produces than in receiving the information that answers its questions. While this thinking is still at an embryonic stage, it underlines the need to consider WHO will produce WHAT at each stage, prior to fee proposals being finalised. This creates a level playing field, may reduce the amount of information produced in the early stages and ensures that the client receives the right amount of information at the end of each stage to allow the project to be signed off and progress to the next stage with greater clarity and certainty.

This topic is discussed further in the Information Exchanges section on page 72 and the level of detail text on page 73.

The client and the Building Contract

The client will have to enter into a Building Contract with a contractor in order to construct the designed project. The degree of detail contained in the Employer's Requirements and the contractor's response (the Contractor's Proposals) will depend on the form of procurement adopted. The exception to this rule is a traditional project, where the contractor will be expected to construct the project as set out in the design team's information, although discrete aspects of the design may be developed by a specialist subcontractor. In some instances the Contractor's Proposals may not be sufficiently developed to enable the Employer's Requirements to be completely disregarded. In these instances, the precedence of information must be clearly established in the Building Contract.

Summary

The project brief is a core design tool, particularly during Stage 2, when it will continue to be refined as the Concept Design develops. However, the inclusion of Project Outcomes and other objectives within the project brief requires the project lead to consider the duties of the various parties in greater detail, particularly for the post-handover and in-use project stages.

6

Chapter

WHO is in the project team?

Every project, whether large or small, requires a number of roles to be undertaken. On smaller projects, roles are typically combined, with the architect carrying out the project lead, lead designer and architect roles. If a practice has the requisite experience, they may also provide cost advice and undertake the contract administrator role. For a project of limited scale, it may not be necessary to utilise the skills of structural or building services engineers, but it will be necessary to appoint a contractor. In its simplest terms, a minimum of three parties are required to deliver a small project.

On larger projects, the opposite is true. It is likely that all of the core project roles will be required (see Figure 6.1). The requirement for these will vary from stage to stage (as set out in Figure 3.1) and it is likely that most roles will be undertaken by different parties. Additional roles (see Figure 6.2) may also be required in order to provide specific advice (for example, in relation to masterplanning, sustainability, landscaping, planning, fire engineering, external lighting, acoustics or catering). There are two further complications:

- certain roles can be fulfilled by different generic organisations – for example, the architectural practice, project management company, cost consultant or an independent specialist company may all have the experience necessary to undertake the health and safety adviser role (further examples and explanation are given later in this chapter)

- there may be benefits in the party carrying out a role changing as the project progresses (examples of when this might occur are detailed on page 59).

The Project Roles Table has been designed to assist with determining the roles that are required on a project at each stage and then deciding on which party should undertake them. Before considering some of the issues associated with these decisions it is important to first consider the relationship between the contractor and the design team.

The relationship between the contractor and the design team

The first decision to be made by the client, in conjunction with the project lead, is whether a traditional or contractor-led project team is to be assembled. This is a core decision as it fundamentally impacts on the procurement of all members of the team and how the project team is assembled.

On smaller projects, this will be a straightforward decision as the majority of such projects still use traditional project teams with the contractor appointed after the design team has completed the design proposals. On some larger schemes, there may be a client or funder preference for contractor-led procurement. In many cases either approach may be acceptable and the pros and cons of each will need to be carefully considered by the client.

Deciding on whether a project team is to be traditional or contractor-led is a core Stage 0 issue in the RIBA Plan of Work 2013 as it impacts on how the Stage 1 team is assembled and what their outputs might be.

Where a traditional team is proposed, or a traditional team that will convert to a contractor-led team via novation of the design team to the contractor, the timing of the contractor's involvement will still influence, and indeed dictate, the roles and responsibilities of certain parties at each stage and is therefore a core decision.

Why is the timing of contractor involvement crucial?

Regardless, of whether a traditional or a contractor-led team is proposed, the precise timing of the contractor's involvement is crucial to assembling the project team. Early contractor involvement:

- allows the earlier involvement of specialist subcontractors

- ensures that buildability and associated health and safety issues are considered

- enables site logistical issues to be considered

- can facilitate a quicker start on site, and

- assists in minimising the contractor's allocation of any risk allowances.

As part of this decision-making process, the timing of the award of the Building Contract is also crucial as it may impact on who is employing the design team at a particular stage and may also flag up the need for another adviser to produce the Construction Strategy or to contribute to the Health and Safety Strategy during the early project stages. Additionally, the timing will influence some of the leadership roles during the key early design stages and design quality considerations.

Setting aside the strategic decision regarding a traditional or contractor-led team at Stage 0, the RIBA Plan of Work 2013 has been conceptually devised in a manner that aligns the involvement of the contractor during Stages 2, 3 or 4 to the commonly used procurement routes included in the bespoke practice- or project-specific RIBA Plan of Work 2013.

Details of these different approaches and the pros and cons of early contractor engagement are set out below.

When deciding on the procurement route to be used (the point at which contractor involvement will occur) the form of Building Contract may also be considered and selected. The form of Building Contract may be influenced by the procurement route and, more importantly, it may influence the choice of professional services contracts for appointing the rest of the project team as part of the procurement strategy. This issue is covered further in Chapter 10.

With the decision regarding a traditional or contractor-led project team made and the timing of the contractor's involvement agreed, the assembly of the project team can be considered in greater detail.

Before proceeding to the consideration of the project roles it is important to remember that the timing of contractor involvement does not necessarily dictate responsibilities for design: traditional procurement results in design responsibility remaining with the designers, although discrete elements of design responsibility may be allocated to the contractor (Performance Specified Work in JCT Building Contracts). Design responsibility is considered in greater detail in Chapter 7.

Timing of contractor involvement

Contractor involvement at the start of Stage 2 – Concept Design
Contractor-led design
If the contractor is to lead the design process, it is essential that they are involved at the start of Stage 2. This is achieved by issuing the Initial Project Brief at the end of Stage 1 as part of the Employer's Requirements documentation to a number of shortlisted contractors. Bids, including design proposals, prepared by each contractor's design team, are submitted at the end of Stage 2. Once these bids have been assessed, a contractor may be appointed in full or on limited terms to develop the design during Stage 3 and prior to conclusion of a Building Contract.

Contractor involvement at the start of Stage 3 – Developed Design
Two-stage design and build/management contracting
In this scenario, tender documents are issued during Stage 2 with a view to appointing a contractor to undertake pre-construction duties prior to the end of Stage 2. This allows the contractor to contribute, where possible, prior to the design process before the end of Stage 2, when initial iterations in relation to the coordinated design are being considered, and to be fully involved during Stages 3 and 4. The Building Contract may be concluded at the end of Stage 3 or during Stage 4, in accordance with the Project Programme.

Contractor involvement at the start of, or during, Stage 4 – Technical Design
Single-stage design and build
In this model the design is tendered using the Stage 3 Information Exchanges and, following the tender process, a contractor is appointed. The contractor is then likely to undertake Stages 4 and 5 simultaneously. There may be a requirement for some aspects of the design team's information, which on other forms of procurement would be produced during Stage 4, to be undertaken at Stage 3 for inclusion in the tender. This can be agreed and incorporated into the Project Programme and the agreed Information Exchanges and included in the Design Responsibility Matrix.

Contractor involvement during Stage 4 – Technical Design
Traditional
The design team completes its information during Stage 4 and issues it for tender. The contractor is appointed during Stage 4 with the specialist subcontractors then carrying out any design work stated in the Building Contract. It is likely that the Stage 4 subcontractor design work would be carried out in parallel with construction (Stage 5).

The pros and cons of early contractor involvement

The advantages of early contractor involvement will depend on the complexity of a project, the nature of the site and the extent to which specialist subcontractors might add value to a project. The positive aspects would be:

- the contractor's supply chain can be involved at an earlier point, in order to harness the knowledge and experience of specialist contractors

- it allows strategies for logistics, health and safety and other considerations to be developed earlier in the design process

- it allows the contractor to better understand (two-stage design and build) or be in better control of (contractor-led procurement) the project risks.

The downsides of early contractor involvement are:

- the client does not have direct access to the designers (contractor-led)

- a larger team is more difficult to manage

- design innovation may be stifled or impeded by designers having to address issues that are not central to the design process.

The timing of contractor involvement establishes the generic nature of the project team. Once this has been determined, the specific roles required at each stage can be considered, decisions regarding the party best placed to undertake each role can be made and the Contractual Tree that links the various parties together developed.

The pros and cons of later contractor involvement

Traditional procurement involves the contractor later than other forms of procurement and the pros and cons are considered in relation to this form of procurement. The advantages are:

- the design team can focus on the design without being unduly influenced by buildability matters, bringing their experience to bear on those issues

- a smaller design team can focus more clearly on core design development and coordination issues.

The downsides are:

- the skills of designing specialist subcontractors are not harnessed early enough in the design process and certainly too late to influence major decisions such as the choice of building frame

- construction risks and site logistics, including buildability, may not be considered in adequate detail at a sufficiently early stage.

The timing of contractor involvement establishes the generic nature of the project team. Once this has been determined, the specific roles required at each stage can be considered, decisions regarding the party best placed to undertake each role can be made and the Contractual Tree developed.

What differentiates the Project Roles Table and the Contractual Tree?

While the consideration of the required project roles is straightforward it does require a number of detailed decisions to be made and a number of strategic points to be addressed. These are covered below. To simplify this decision-making process, the RIBA Plan of Work 2013 advocates the preparation of two documents: the Project Roles Table and the Contractual Tree. The Project Roles Table establishes which roles are required on a project at each stage. The Contractual Tree sets out the contractual relationships between the parties allocated to carry out each role.

By separating these aspects, a simple diagram can be used to represent the Contractual Tree. Both documents can be developed either in succession or simultaneously. The crucial point is that if the simple steps to determine WHO is to be involved are not properly carried out, the next steps, which require more time, will not be as effective. More importantly, the same Project Roles Table can work with different Contractual Trees. By separating the two diagrams, the complexity of the decision-making processes is simplified.

What project roles are required?

The first step in the preparation of the Project Roles Table is to consider the roles that are required on a project. Unless the project is limited in its nature and scope – for example, undertaking work up to the application for planning consent only – all of the core project roles will be required (see Figure 6.1).

The need for additional roles will depend on the specific demands of each project, as well as the skill sets of the core designers, and it may be necessary to revisit the need for these roles as the project progresses. However, early scoping of these roles can be important in ensuring that adequate fee allowances are made by the client, as well as assisting in the preparation of detailed Schedules of Services, allocating design responsibility and agreeing Information Exchanges.

Once all of the necessary roles have been determined, the possibilities of combining roles, consideration of who might undertake them at each stage and the circumstances in which particular roles may not be required at certain stages can be considered.

Figure 6.1

Core project roles

Role	Principal duties of core roles
Client	The party commissioning the design and construction of a project. The client may be an individual or a company. In the latter case, an individual should act as a single point of responsibility for decisions and communication even if numerous bodies, or individuals, within the client organisation will contribute to decisions. The client may use a RIBA Client Adviser, a specially accredited individual, able to provide strategic advice in the early stages of a project in relation to the strategic definition or briefing aspects as well as the best methods for setting up the project team.
Client adviser	A consultant providing strategic or specialist advice particularly during the early project stages.
Project lead	The party responsible for managing all aspects of the project and ensuring that the project is delivered in accordance with the Project Programme.
Lead designer	The party responsible for managing all aspects of the design, including the coordination of the design and the integration of specialist subcontractors' design, where applicable, into the coordinated design.
Construction lead	The party responsible for constructing the project and for providing construction advice in the early stages. The contractor would be the construction lead at Stage 5. This role has been introduced to provide flexibility regarding who performs this role prior to work commencing on site.
Architect	Responsible for carrying out the architectural design.
Civil and structural engineer	Responsible for carrying out the structural engineering design. On larger projects civil engineering aspects would be undertaken by this role.
Building services engineer	Responsible for carrying out the building services design.
Cost consultant	The party responsible for producing Cost Information as the design progresses. This information will vary depending on the project but may include the overall Project Budget, estimates of the construction cost and life cycle cost analysis.
Contract administrator	The party responsible for the administration of the Building Contract, including issuing of additional instructions and the various certificates required to allow the handover and occupation of a building, until all of the defects have been rectified and the defect period concluded.
Health and safety adviser	Responsible for health and safety aspects as defined by legislation and in line with other project objectives and health and safety best practice.

Figure 6.2

Additional project roles

Role	Principal duties of additional roles
Acoustic consultant	Provides specialist acoustic advice on particular projects in relation to sound quality in spaces or noise transfer between rooms or from the external environment.
Archaeologist	Undertakes desktop and site investigations to comply with any requirement of the planning consent.
BREEAM assessor	Carries out BREEAM assessments.
Cladding specialist	Undertakes specialist design and/or reviews of aspects of the external cladding of a building, particularly where bespoke solutions are proposed.
Catering consultant	Provides strategic and briefing catering advice as well as specific designs derived from the final catering brief.
Access consultant issues.	Provides specialist advice in relation to disabled and other access
Facilities management (FM) adviser	Reviews the design proposals and comments on facilities management and in-use maintenance matters.
Fire engineer	Provides fire engineering advice in relation to fire engineered solutions and/or advice in relation to fire aspects of the Building Regulations.
Highways consultant	Provides strategic advice on the implications of a design on the adjacent road network and may provide travel plans, transport assessments or other road-related information.
Information manager	Manages the flow of information between parties – note that this is not a design role.
Interior designer	Provides particular design services in relation to the interior design of a project.
Landscape architect	Responsible for carrying out the landscape design.
Lighting designer	Provides specialist lighting advice internally or in relation to the floodlighting and external lighting of a project.
Masterplanner	Provides specialist advice for larger sites in relation to planning, roads, social issues and other high-level strategies.
Operational lead	Responsible for the facilities management (FM) aspects of the building.
Party wall surveyor	Provides specialist advice in relation to adjacent properties and issues such as right of light.
Planning consultant	Provides specialist advice in relation to planning applications.
Security adviser	Considers security issues in relation to the design of a building and may assist with certain briefing aspects.
Signage designer	Provides wayfinding strategies and the design of the corresponding
Sustainability adviser	Provides strategic advice in relation to green issues.
Technical adviser	A consultant employed by the client to provide specific advice, particularly on design and build or contractor-led procurement routes.

How are project roles allocated?

The allocation of project roles to specific parties is a crucial consideration, regardless of project size, and this cannot be emphasised enough. Where a practice is following the steps outlined in this publication to prepare practice-specific documents that will be used time and time again, this step is important as any issues might arise repeatedly on a number of projects before appropriate adjustments to a practice's documentation can be made.

While preparation of the Project Roles Table can be undertaken in parallel with preparing the Contractual Tree (which is considered next) there are advantages to preparing them in isolation: decisions are not clouded by the need to consider contractual relationships. In either case, the result is different but complementary outputs: a Project Roles Table and a Contractual Tree(s) or organogram(s).

With the required project roles determined and agreed and the timing of contractor involvement settled, preparation of the Project Roles Table considers which party is best placed to undertake each role at each stage. There are three factors that influence this decision:

- certain roles are typically combined or allocated to a single party

- roles may pass from one party to another as the project, and stages, progress

- a project may be limited in its scope.

These factors are now considered.

What roles might be combined?

It is common for one party to be appointed to undertake a number of roles. Common scenarios include:

- an architectural practice undertaking the lead designer, architect and contract administrator roles

- a project management company undertaking the project lead as well as the cost consultant role

- the building services engineer carrying out the lead designer role on a complex engineering project such as a data centre, or the civil engineer on an infrastructure project

- a major consultancy practice undertaking the structural and building services engineering roles as well as some of the secondary roles, such as acoustics and fire engineering, and

- a cost consultancy undertaking the cost consultant and health and safety adviser roles.

In this guidance, it is not possible to dwell on who is best placed to undertake each role as there are many factors that may dictate the final decision. However, it is worth mentioning that the relationship between the project lead, lead designer and construction lead and the ability of those carrying out these roles to work collaboratively are fundamental to the success of a project and these roles require particular and careful consideration.

When should roles pass from one organisation to another?

There are a number of scenarios where a specific role might be undertaken by a different party at each stage. For example:

- a client adviser may undertake the architect role at Stages 0 and 1, with a different architect appointed to develop the Concept Design at Stage 2

- one architectural practice may carry out the Concept Design (Stage 2) and another the Developed Design and Technical Design (Stages 3 and 4)

- on a traditional contract, the project lead, the lead designer or a specialist construction adviser might undertake the construction lead during Stages 2 to 4, prior to the contractor being appointed, and

- the contractor's specialist subcontractor might assume M&E designer responsibilities during Stage 4 and develop the design produced by the mechanical services designer during Stage 3, depending on the contractual circumstances.

Again, it is not possible to consider who is best placed to perform a particular role at a particular stage as this will depend on how the client wishes to assemble the project team and on the skill sets of the various parties. The greatest aggregation is likely to occur on smaller projects and it is important that those considering undertaking a number of roles ensure that they have the appropriate skills to match the roles' requirements. The increasing number of claims arising from contract administration or planning applications duties underlines this point.

What stages are being commissioned?

It is important to consider the stages applicable to a project and also which role is required at each stage. The former is relevant where the client wishes to appoint the team to undertake limited services: for example, up to planning application at Stage 2 or 3. The latter is of equal importance as acquiring too many project team members too quickly makes for a cumbersome team that is difficult to manage. Of course, the converse is true and late input from one party can result in changes to the design in later stages.

Using the Project Roles Table

The Project Roles Table has been developed to allow the party responsible for developing the project team with the client to allocate each project role to a specific party for each stage (bearing in mind the three points raised above). The Project Roles Table will typically be generated before the majority of parties have been appointed and it is therefore intended that the table is updated on a regular basis with the generic titles utilised by the practice or contractor replaced by the actual names of the appointed parties.

Of course, on smaller projects the table might be seen as a 'sledgehammer to crack a nut'. In the large and small project examples that are set out below it can be seen that the Project Roles Table is a valuable tool even on smaller projects. It underlines the number of roles being undertaken by the architect as well as clarifying the other parties involved at each stage, although some may decide that a Contractual Tree is sufficient for advising the client. It needs to be remembered that the RIBA Plan of Work 2013 is a guidance document aligned to a flexible kit of parts that can be used in the most appropriate way to ensure the accurate definition of the Project Team, whether a project is large or small, simple or complex.

Before analysing the two examples that are now set out, it is crucial to remember that, while the contractual relationships may be considered during the preparation of this table, it is the Contractual Tree (examples shown on pages 64 and 66 for the same two projects) that clarifies the contractual relationship between each party involved in the project team.

The examples in **Figures 6.3** and **6.4** show only the core project roles. The online tool available at www.ribaplanofwork.com/toolbox enables the creation of a project- or practice-specific Project Roles Table. A bespoke table can be extended to include any additional project roles that are required and additional guidance on completing a Project Roles Table is also available from this website.

RIBA Project Roles Table – large project

The example of the Project Roles Table set out in **Figure 6.3** is typical of what would be expected after the project lead has considered the points set out in this section with the client.

Figure 6.3 Example of a large Project Roles Table

Role/Stage	0	1	2	3	4	5	6	7
Client	P1	P1	P1	P1	P1	P1	P1	P1
Client adviser	P2	P2	NR	NR	P6	P6	P6	NR
Project lead	NR	P3	P3	P3	P3	P3	P3	NR
Lead designer	NR	NR	P4	P4	P4	P4	P4	NR
Architect	P2	P2	P4	P4	P4	P4	P4	P4
Civil and structural engineer	NR	NR	P5	P5	P5	P5	P5	NR
Building services engineer	NR	NR	P6	P6	P6	P8	P8	NR
Cost consultant	P7	P7	P7	P7	P7	P7	P7	NR
Construction lead	NR	NR	P3	P3	P8	P8	P8	NR
Contract administrator	NR	NR	NR	P7	P7	P7	P7	NR
Health and safety adviser	NR	P3	P3	P3	P3	P3	P3	NR

List of parties involved in project
P1 = Party 1 – Big Widget Ltd (client)
P2 = Party 2 – Sam Wilson (RIBA Client Adviser)
P3 = Party 3 – Big City PM (project management company)
P4 = Party 4 – Architectural practice
P5 = Party 5 – Structural engineering practice
P6 = Party 6 – Building services practice
P7 = Party 7 – Cost consultant practice
P8 = Party 8 – Contractor
P9 = Party 9 – FM specialist

NR = Role not required during this stage.

From the worked example in **Figure 6.3**, the following points can be gleaned:

- The client adviser (at Stage 0) and project lead (at Stage 1) have already been appointed and are therefore named, along with the client, in the list accompanying the table.

- A RIBA Client Adviser was appointed for Stage 0 to assist in the strategic definition of the project and advise on the preparation of the Initial Project Brief during Stage 1 and is allocated the architect's role for these stages.

- Single-stage design and build was determined as the procurement route and the contractor will therefore be involved from the commencement of Stage 4.

- An architectural practice is to be appointed from Stage 2 onwards and will also carry out the lead designer role.

- The project lead and health and safety adviser roles are to be aggregated and will be carried out by a project management company.

- The cost consultant will also be undertaking the contract administrator role.

RIBA Project Roles Table – small project

The example of the Project Roles Table in **Figure 6.4** is typical of what would be expected after the project lead has considered the points set out in this section with the client.

Figure 6.4 Example of a small Project Roles Table

Role/Stage	0	1	2	3	4	5	6	7
Client	P1	P1	P1	P1	P1	P1	P1	NR
Client adviser	NR	NR	NR	NR	NR	NR	NR	NR
Project lead	P2	P2	P2	P2	P2	P2	P2	NR
Lead designer	NR	NR	P2	P2	P2	P2	P2	NR
Architect	P2	P2	P2	P2	P2	P2	P2	NR
Civil and structural engineer	NR	NR	P4	P4	P4	P4	P4	NR
Building services engineer	NR	NR	NR	P6	P6	NR	NR	NR
Cost consultant	NR	P5	P5	P2	P2	P2	P2	NR
Construction lead	NR	NR	P2	P2	P3	P3	P3	NR
Contract administrator	NR	NR	NR	NR	P2	P2	P2	NR
Health and safety adviser	NR	P7	P7	P7	P7	P7	P7	NR

List of parties involved in project
P1 = Party 1 – Mr and Mrs Client
P2 = Party 2 – City Centre Architects (architectural practice)
P3 = Party 3 – Contractor
P4 = Party 4 – Big Beam Ltd (civil and structural engineering practice)
P5 = Party 5 – Clear Costs LLP (cost consultant)
P6 = Party 6 – Wires & Fires Ltd (building services engineer)
P7 = Party 7 – Safety Ensured Ltd (health and safety consultant)

NR = Role not required during this stage.

From the worked example in **Figure 6.4**, the following points can be gleaned:

- City Centre Architects is undertaking the project lead, lead designer, architect and contract administrator roles.

- City Centre Architects will be undertaking the construction lead role in Stages 2 and 3 inclusive, prior to the appointment of the contractor.

- Clear Costs LLP will be preparing Cost Information at Stages 1 and 2; however, City Centre Architects will take over the cost management after this stage as part of their contract administrator role.

- The nature of the project requires a building services engineer to assist only with the Developed Design and the preparation of Technical Design information.

- Big Beam Ltd are appointed for Stages 2 to 6 inclusive, allowing them to produce their Technical Design information, carry out site inspections on the structural works and assist on site, as required.

- Safety Ensured Ltd will be undertaking the health and safety adviser role from Stage 1 onwards.

- There are no Stage 7 duties when the building will be in use.

Establishing the Contractual Tree

As highlighted in the last section, the preparation of the Contractual Tree can be undertaken when the Project Roles Table is being completed and the two are intrinsically linked. They have, however, been kept as two distinct activities due to the different outputs that are created. There can also be benefits in considering the project roles in isolation from contractual issues.

The Contractual Tree is prepared using the parties identified in the Project Roles Table. One Contractual Tree should be sufficient for the majority of projects, although where a design and build contract is utilised a second Contractual Tree may be required to clarify any contractual changes (for example, novation) even though the parties involved may remain the same (see **Figures 6.5** and **6.6**).

When preparing the Contractual Tree, consideration can also be given to how each party will be procured and appointed as part of the broader procurement strategy. For example, fee proposals, competitive interviews or invited competition are some of the methods that might be used to appoint the architect. Certain decisions will be required at Stage 0 and, as part of the initial considerations for assembling the project team, there may be advantages in producing an initial Contractual Tree.

Some consultants may be appointed as subconsultants to other consultants and this consideration is an essential element in the preparation of this document. Indeed, it would be possible to generate a number of Contractual Trees for the same Project Roles Table.

On the following pages, examples of the Contractual Trees that match the Project Roles Tables set out in **Figures 6.3** and **6.4** are illustrated. To underline the previous point, it can be seen in the large project example that if the client were to appoint the structural engineer directly it would result in a different Contractual Tree without impacting on the Project Roles Table.

A Contractual Tree can be prepared using different means and therefore no templates are necessary or provided in this publication.

The Contractual Tree and Project Roles Table are simple but extremely important documents. They require close consideration and act as the backbone for the preparation of more detailed appointment documents and the related appendices, which are considered next.

Contractual Tree: large project

Figure 6.5 Large project Contractual Tree – Stages 1 to 3

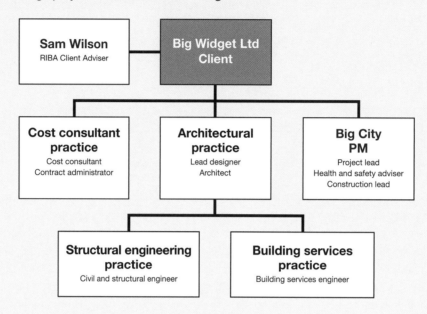

Figure 6.6 Large project Contractual Tree – Stages 4 to 6 following novation of design team members to the contractor

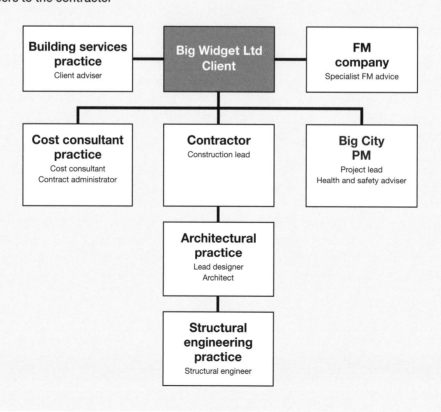

From the worked examples of a Contractual Tree in **Figures 6.5** and **6.6,** the following points can be gleaned:

- Sam Wilson and Big City PM are the only appointed parties at the point the Contractual Tree was prepared.

- The cost consultant, architect and Big City PM will be appointed directly by the client.

- The structural engineering and building services engineer are to be appointed as subconsultants to the architectural practice during Stages 1 to 3.

- The building services engineer will not be novated to the contractor.

- The contractual complexities related to the design and build procurement route are clearly illustrated and the contractual transition from Stage 3 to Stage 4 is clear.

- The complexities of any additional roles are omitted for clarity.

Contractual Tree: small project

Figure 6.7 Small project Contractual Tree based on Figure 6.4 Project Roles Table

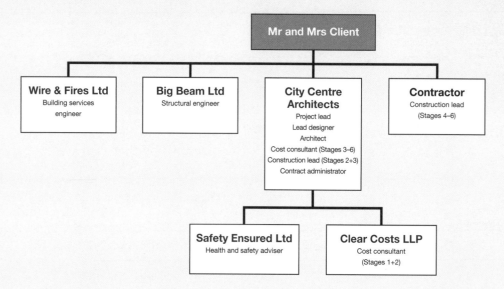

From the worked example of a Contractual Tree in **Figure 6.7**, the following points can be gleaned:

- City Centre Architects are undertaking the majority of the project roles.

- Wires & Fires Ltd and Big Beam Ltd will be appointed directly by the client.

- City Centre Architects will contract directly with the cost consultant and the health and safety adviser.

- The cost consultant and construction lead roles transfer between parties and this has been clarified.

- From the Project Roles Table (**Figure 6.4**) it can be seen that Wires & Fires Ltd and Big Beam Ltd are not involved at every stage. It is not necessary to clarify this in the diagram as they are the only parties undertaking their respective roles.

- At the time of preparing the Contractual Tree, the contractor is the only party that has not been identified.

Summary

By carefully considering the roles that are required on a project at each stage and who is best placed to undertake them, along with the core decision on how and when the contractor will be engaged, it is possible to prepare the Project Roles Table and the Contractual Tree. The processes involved aim to ensure that these outputs are carefully considered and robust. This allows detailed Schedules of Services, Information Exchanges and design responsibilities to be considered in greater detail. These are examined in the next chapter.

Chapter

WHAT does the project team need to do?

Chapter overview

With the project roles required at each stage allocated as part of the HOW process, this chapter considers the detailed documents that are necessary to ensure that each party is aware of WHAT they have to do at each stage and that those with design responsibilities are clear about what they have to design. More importantly, by considering these tasks collectively, in a multidisciplinary manner, there is less likelihood of overlaps or gaps in the overall services required by the client. By properly scheduling the tasks to be undertaken and the information to be exchanged at the end of each stage, the client can be confident that the project team has been properly assembled and the design team can be satisfied that their fee agreements reflect WHAT they will do. The project lead and lead designer can also be certain that any duties required to be fulfilled by other members of the project team in order to meet their own obligations are properly considered.

With the core strategic diagrams (Project Roles Table and Contractual Tree) properly considered, prepared and agreed with the client, the detailed documents required to define WHAT each party will do can be prepared. Assembling the project team requires the preparation of two core documents:

- a **Design Responsibility Matrix** incorporating Information Exchanges, and

- **Multidisciplinary Schedules of Services**.

The Design Responsibility Matrix considers the design interface between the various designers in the design team and the specialist subcontractors appointed by the contractor. This document is an important starting point as it creates clarity in terms of design responsibilities. Information Exchanges are an important new subject covered by the RIBA Plan of Work 2013 and consider the information that will be exchanged with the client at the end of each stage. This information can impact on the fees for each designer and, as the work of one designer influences the work of others, particularly during the early and more iterative stages, the lead designer may need to factor into the fee proposal the fees required to deliver coordinated information at Stage 3 or integrated information at Stage 4. Schedules of Services also have to be prepared to align with the Handover Strategy and any requirements of the Building Contract and to accurately reflect the additional management tasks required to assist with matters such as Risk Assessments. The purpose of the two documents is covered next.

A project- or practice-specific Design Responsibility Matrix incorporating Information Exchanges can be prepared using the formats set out in **Figures 7.1** to **7.3** with sample Schedules of Services set out in the appendix. Alternatively, all documents can be prepared using the online tools available at www.ribaplanofwork.com/toolbox.

What is the purpose of a Design Responsibility Matrix?

Determining whether a traditional or contractor-led project team is more appropriate and establishing the timing of the contractor's involvement influences the proposed procurement route and the form of Building Contract to be used. These, in turn, dictate whether the contractor will be contractually responsible for any design work. The options for responsibility comprise:

- no design work

- discrete aspects of the design, or

- all aspects of the design.

However, regardless of the procurement route and the contractual allocation of design responsibility to the contractor, the actual design work will be undertaken by either a member of the design team or a specialist subcontractor. Projects where the design team is fully responsible for all aspects of the design are increasingly rare (except perhaps smaller projects). It is therefore likely that certain aspects of the design will be progressed by a member of the design team to a predetermined level of detail and then completed by a specialist subcontractor prior to fabrication and construction (curtain walling, for example) whereas other aspects (such as brickwork) will be developed by a member of the design team in sufficient detail to enable construction on site.

The Design Responsibility Matrix considers this crucial point and is used to allocate design responsibility for each aspect of a project to a member of the design team, as well as setting out which aspects will be developed by a specialist subcontractor. The matrix assists by defining the design boundaries between design team members as well as the items that will be developed by a specialist subcontractor. The matrix can then be used to define the extent of design work to be included in the Contractor's Designed Portion of a JCT Building Contract, which is a recognised method of allocating design responsibility for discrete aspects of the design to a contractor on traditional contracts. A further complexity is determining how the various elements will be specified. This may impact on the specialist subcontractors selected by the contractor to tender for the works and can have a fundamental effect on other aspects, such as the contractor's ability to employ innovative solutions or have greater control over the specification of materials.

It is, of course, difficult to apportion precise aspects of the design before a design exists; however, the Design Responsibility Matrix allows responsibility to be defined generically at the start of the project, based on experience gained from previous projects. The matrix can then be revisited as the design progresses and adjusted to reflect any changes to design responsibility that may be necessary.

Although, on the whole, designers are aware of the aspects of the design for which they will be responsible, certain aspects might justifiably be undertaken by a number of designers. Furthermore, for the majority of building elements there is no defined or industry-wide agreement that clarifies where the boundary between the designers and the specialist subcontractors lies. The Design Responsibility Matrix seeks to bring clarity on these matters early on in a project, allowing responsibility to be discussed, any ambiguities to be resolved and the broad-brush principles agreed. For example:

- the architect may have responsibility for determining the ceiling grid dimensions, the building services engineer responsibility for the light fittings and air grilles and the specialist subcontractor responsibility for designing the support up to the structure, taking into account the services above

- the building services engineer may have responsibility for designing the area of gutter required and routing the pipework to connect with the substructure drainage designed by the civil and structural engineer, with the roofing specialist subcontractor responsible for detailing the gutter and the architect determining the interface with the parapet.

These are two straightforward examples and they are not proposed as the optimum solution, but merely serve to highlight the design complexity of certain items and the need for clarity regarding them. Producing the matrix, and clarifying design responsibilities at an early stage, achieves a number of goals:

- it ensures that each designer is clear about their design responsibilities and the level of detail to be achieved for each aspect they are designing (via Information Exchanges), enabling their drawings and specifications or information to be prepared accordingly

- it ensures that Stage 4 information is developed appropriately by design team members (i.e. the appropriate design required to suit a performance, full: generic or full: proprietary level of detail; see the boxed example)

- it makes certain that the contractor is aware of any design responsibility obligations to be included in the Building Contract

- it allows fees to be properly apportioned and considered by each party

- it reduces any ambiguities about responsibilities, minimising the possibilities of disputes later in the design process when the project team is likely to be working 'flat out'.

For smaller practitioners that frequently work with the same structural engineer or other designers, and that perhaps use the same products and/or assemblies from project to project, the Design Responsibility Matrix can be generated based on a practice's usual working methods and then used on successive projects. A practice Design Responsibility Matrix ensures that any design responsibility being allocated to the contractor is clear from the outset to all members of the design team, helps to inform the inexperienced client and can be adjusted in line with project Feedback.

The use of BIM does not remove the need to agree a Design Responsibility Matrix. In fact, the reverse is true: an integrated and collaborative team must be fully aware of WHO is designing WHAT.

Full versus performance specification

One crucial reason for creating a Design Responsibility Matrix is that the decision on whether or not a specialist subcontractor is to 'take over' the development of an aspect of the building dictates the level of detail to which the geometric information will be developed (see page 80) and also whether the specification will be developed fully or on a performance basis. With the latter, the design team members determine a product or solution that will be used and produce a prescriptive solution, and their information, accordingly. This is defined as 'full: proprietary' in the Design Responsibility Matrix. However, an option exists to set all of the appropriate standards so that the contractor still has the ability to determine the final choice of product. This option (full: generic) is more commonplace on design and build forms of Building Contract and the client may require the selections to be vetted. With a performance specification, the performance criteria are set out by the design team, giving the specialist subcontractor a degree of flexibility in developing the design solution. The Level of Design section of the Design Responsibility Matrix deals with this issue. One further complexity is that, even where the design team is designing to full: proprietary, the specialist contractor may have to produce 'shop drawings' for off-site fabrication purposes.

To the majority of clients, the Design Responsibility Matrix may be unimportant; however, when this document is prepared early on they can be assured that design team fees are being apportioned appropriately. The lead designer needs to pay particular attention to the Design Responsibility Matrix as the matrix may impact on their ability to perform their role.

A template Design Responsibility Matrix and two examples derived from a large and small project are set out in **Figure 7.1** and **Figures 7.2** and **7.3** respectively. These examples include only a limited number of elements to demonstrate the principles of the document. A more comprehensive project- or practice-specific Design Responsibility Matrix can be completed at www.ribaplanofwork.com/toolbox where further advice and information on how to complete the document is available.

Finally, the Design Responsibility Matrix is a core contractual document as it sets the boundaries of the design work between design team members for inclusion within the professional services contracts. Importantly, it can be used to ensure that design is apportioned appropriately in the Building Contract where the Contractor's Designed Portion is being used on a traditional Building Contract. More crucially, even where a design and build or contractor-led form of procurement is being adopted, it is an essential document to bring clarity regarding the design interface between design team members and the specialist subcontractors.

What are Information Exchanges and why are they important?

As a design progresses, the amount of information produced by each design team member, and its level of detail, increases. This is reflected in the information that is exchanged during each stage. This information is used to:

- allow the client to review, comment and sign off the design as it progresses

- permit planning applications, or other statutory approvals, to be submitted

- communicate developing designs to design team members

- enable utilities suppliers, and other third parties, to provide advice or information or to comment on design proposals

- comply with the QA (quality assurance) procedures of a particular party

- assist in the production of cost estimates, and

- enable contractors, and their subcontractors, to tender for the work.

Defining the information to be exchanged is a crucial project requirement because it ensures that:

- each designer produces the right information at the right time

- the information produced is prepared to the correct level of detail for its intended purpose

- the lead designer has the relevant information to coordinate the design work of the design team and integrate the design work of the specialist subcontractors

- the client has the appropriate information to enable the plain language questions to be answered at each stage, and

- the cost consultant and contractor have the appropriate information to cost the emerging design and its corresponding risks.

Information Exchanges can be categorised as follows:

- informal 'work-in-progress' information issued between design team members to allow each designer to progress their own design work, to facilitate collaborative working and to allow the lead designer to coordinate the developing design. This work is typically issued in accordance with a Design Programme

- ad hoc information released to progress a particular topic with third parties (those not included in the project team); for example, seeking comments on a road junction from the local authority or obtaining a ruling from a utilities company on whether the electricity grid is able to accommodate a specific power load

- formal Information Exchanges, which can have a number of functions but are principally a pause in the design process allowing a period for reflection and sign-off by the client before the next stage commences.

In this guidance, the first two categories are not examined in detail although they are touched on briefly in the WHEN (programme) and HOW (protocol) sections. Formal Information Exchanges are, however, worth considering. The means of defining Information Exchanges (the information exchanged at the end of each stage and its level of detail) is one of the crucial topics to emerge from the development of the RIBA Plan of Work 2013. It is fair to say that the information currently produced at the end of a RIBA stage varies from project to project and from practice to practice. This variation can occur for good reasons: for example, one residential client may want only a set of drawings for obtaining planning and building control approvals. Another may need detailed interior designs and full-size joinery details. Some may require fly-through videos, models and sophisticated renderings in order to sign off the Concept Design at Stage 2. Certain Information Exchanges are likely to be dictated: the requirements of a specific planning authority or the information required to confirm compliance with Building Regulations, for example.

In summary, the information that needs to be exchanged during a stage and the information that needs to be delivered at the end of a stage varies and is dictated by a number of factors. The information and level of detail to be produced by each designer needs to be considered at Stage 1 as it can impact on fee proposals. From the lead designer's perspective, the information to be delivered by each designer during each stage is important and it is essential that those undertaking this role produce a Design Programme that clarifies what is expected, WHEN, and HOW cost exercises will be undertaken.

Information Exchanges are incorporated into the Design Responsibility Matrix. The Schedule of Services, Design Programme and the Design Responsibility Matrix provide a comprehensive kit of parts for those undertaking the lead designer role. The Information Exchanges columns in the Design Responsibility Matrix are straightforward and allow the drawings, schedules, strategies and other information that must be exchanged at the end of each stage to be identified. Specifically, they do not define a detailed drawing list, but rather provide a broad understanding of what is to be produced at each stage and to what 'scale' or level of detail (see below). The multidisciplinary nature of the Design Responsibility Matrix is also useful for the lead designer. From their perspective, it is essential that the other designers are appointed in a manner that allows them to undertake their coordination duties. In summary, the Matrix:

- defines the information that will be exchanged at end of each stage

- clarifies which party will produce the information, and

- defines the scale or level of detail to be produced.

RIBA Design Responsibility Matrix incorporating Information Exchanges

How to use the Design Responsibility Matrix

Figure. 7.1 RIBA Design Responsibility Matrix incorporating Information Exchanges

		3. Developed Design			4. Technical Design				4. Technical Design					
Aspect of design		Design team			Design team				Contractor			Building Contract		
Uniclass ref.	Element	Design Resp.	LOD	Info. Exch.	Design Resp.	LOD	Info. Exch.		Design Resp.	LOD	Info. Exch.	CDP	Warr.	Note
1	2	3	4	5	6	7	8		9	10	11	12	13	14

Note: For clarity, Stage 2 is not shown in this example

The Design Responsibility Matrix incorporates the Information Exchanges to be made at the end of each stage. The purpose of allocating design responsibility and defining Information Exchanges has been set out on the previous pages. This figure clarifies the specific purpose of each column of the Design Responsibility Matrix. A practice- or project-specific Design Responsibility Matrix can be generated using in-house templates based on the format and logic set out in this figure

or a template can be downloaded from www.ribaplanofwork. com/toolbox. It is intended that the online template should continue to evolve in line with feedback and that the template will be developed into an online tool. It is crucial to read the Level of Design (LOD) columns and the Information Exchange columns together as LOD may dictate that an outline specification is required whereas the Information Exchange may require no geometric information to be exchanged.

Function of each column

Column 1
This reference is derived from the elements table (EE) of Uniclass 2.

Column 2
This is the element/system of the building for which design responsibility is being allocated.

Columns 3, 6 and 9
Design Responsibility: this is the party that is responsible for this aspect of design at this stage.

Columns 4, 7 and 10
Level of Design (LOD): the column clarifies the Level of Design that will be produced at a given stage. While the terms are primarily specification orientated, it is expected that the level of detail in any 2D or 3D geometric information in the Information Exchanges will reflect the Level of Design that is produced. The different levels of design are:

Outline (Out): This level of design should be sufficient to enable the client to sign off the proposals and to allow the appropriate Cost Information to be produced.

Performance (P): The design is progressed on a performance basis with the specialist subcontractor developing the design in accordance with the performance criteria set out. The geometric information should be developed accordingly.

Full: generic (F-G): The full design is completed but the choice of final products is left to the contractor and the appropriate specialist subcontractor.

Full: proprietary (F-P): The full design is completed and specific products are specified.

In some instances, a mixture of levels of design will be required for an assembly. For example, planning requirements may dictate that the brickwork and window components are specified as full: proprietary whereas the 'non-visible' aspects, such as lintels or the inner leaf construction and insulation, are specified as full: generic, allowing best value products to be sourced and proposed by the contractor and the specialist subcontractor.

Columns 5, 8 and 11
Information Exchange: this column is used to confirm what aspects will be included in the Information Exchange at the end of a stage. It can be used to specify the scale of the 2D deliverables that will be produced or, by using 'Yes' or 'No', to clarify whether information on a particular element will be included in the geometric aspect of the 2D or 3D models being produced. This column is primarily associated with geometric information and it is likely that level of detail references will be inserted here once these have been developed in a manner suitable for use industry wide.

Column 12
This column is for use on a JCT traditional form of contract using the Contractor's Designed Portion (CDP) to allocate discrete aspects of the design to the contractor within the Building Contract. It can be deleted for design and build or contractor-led forms of procurement.

Column 13
This column is for use on larger projects where the client may wish a warranty (Warr.) to be put in place between one of the specialist subcontractors and another party. It can be used for the development of the Building Contract by stipulating the circumstances in which such warranties are required.

Column 14
The Design Responsibility Matrix cannot deal with the complexity of the many design interfaces encountered on a project. To bring further clarity, notes can be added on certain subjects. Examples of these notes are shown in the worked examples in Figures 7.2 and 7.3.

RIBA Design Responsibility Matrix incorporating Information Exchanges

Example one: large project

Figure 7.2 Sample from a large project Design Responsibility Matrix

Aspect of design		2. Concept Design — Design team			3. Developed Design — Design team			4. Technical Design — Design team			4. Technical Design — Contractor			Building Contract		Note
Uniclass ref.	Element	Design Resp.	LOD	Info. Exch.	Design Resp.	LOD	Info. Exch.	Design Resp.	LOD	Info. Exch.	Design Resp.	LOD	Info. Exch.	CDP	Warr.	
	Substructure	D2	Out	N/A	D2	Out	1:100	D2	F-P	1:10	N/A	N/A	N/A	No	No	
	Frame/upper slabs – steel	D2	Out	N/A	D2	Out	1:100	D2	F-G	1:100	C0	F-P	1:100	Yes	Yes	1
	Fire protection	D1	Out	N/A	D1	Out	1:100	D1	P	N/A	C0	F-P	N/A	No	No	
	Stairs (precast)	D2	Out	N/A	D2	Out	1:100	D2	P	1:20	C0	F-P	1:5	Yes	No	
	Brickwork/blockwork	D1	Out	1:100	D1	Out	1:100	D1	F-G	1:5	N/A	N/A	N/A	No	No	2
	Masonry support	D1	Out	N/A	D1	Out	1:100	D1	P	1:5	C0	F-P	1:5	Yes	No	
	Curtain walling	D1	Out	1:100	D1	Out	1:100	D1	P	1:20	C0	F-P	1:5	Yes	Yes	3
	Insulated render	D1	Out	1:100	D1	Out	1:100	D1	F-P	1:5	N/A	N/A	N/A	No	Yes	
	Stone cladding	D1	Out	1:100	D1	Out	1:100	D1	P	1:5	C0	F-P	1:5	Yes	Yes	4
	Louvres	D1	Out	1:100	D1	Out	1:100	D1	P	1:5	N/A	N/A	N/A	No	No	
	Hot and cold water services	D3	Out	N/A	D3	Out	1:100	D3	F-G	1:100	N/A	N/A	N/A	No	Yes	
	Ventilation (natural and a/c)	D3	Out	N/A	D3	Out	1:100	D3	P	1:100	N/A	N/A	N/A	No	Yes	
	Sprinklers	D3	Out	N/A	D3	Out	N/A	D3	P	N/A	C0	F-P	1:100	Yes	Yes	5
	Electrical services	D3	Out	N/A	D3	Out	N/A	D3	F-P	N/A	N/A	N/A	N/A	No	Yes	
	Lifts	D3	Out	N/A	D3	Out	1:100	D3	P	1:20	C0	F-P	1:20	Yes	Yes	

List of parties with design responsibility

D1 = Great Concept Architect
D2 = Solid Foundation Engineers
D3 = Well Fired Mechanical Engineers
C0 = Contractor

Note 1 A number of exposed connections are required for the entrance canopy and will be prepared by D2 for discussion and development with D1.

Note 2 The majority of the specification will be developed on the basis of F-G with certain visible elements required to ensure compliance with planning conditions specified and developed as F-P.

Note 3 A number of double height areas of curtain walling require coordination between D1 and D2 to ensure that the tender properly reflects steelwork requirements.

Note 4 This is developed as a performance (P) package but the stone to be used will be F-P in order to satisfy client and planning requirements.

Note 5 D1 to confirm grid requirements that might take precedence over BS requirements in D3 specification.

This example is not representative of all of the elements of a large project but provides sufficient examples and notes to clarify how the Design Responsibility Matrix should be completed. From this limited worked example, produced at Stage 1 and updated at the beginning of Stage 3, the following points can be observed:

- The detailed notes reflect the enhanced level of design expected at Stage 3. The full team has been specified and each party's design responsibilities noted. The project is to be tendered as a two-stage design and build form of Building Contract and therefore the contractor is generically named.

- Planning discussions and the resultant conditions attached to the planning consent have dictated that a number of items in the external elevation are specified as 'full: proprietary' in order to ensure that samples which have been signed off are adhered to. The 'non-visible' aspects of these elements have, however, been specified in a way that allows the contractor and specialist contractor a degree of flexibility in the design development.

- There are a number of design issues in relation to the steelwork for an entrance canopy and the curtain walling. The responsibilities reflect the coordination work required to ensure that these aspects are properly considered prior to the specialist subcontractors commencing their design work.

- The sprinklers will be performance specified; however, notes 5 clarifies the fact that the tender constraints must consider the ceiling grid dimensions as well as any parameters set out in the building services specification.

- The Information Exchanges at Stage 2 were included in the matrix at Stage 1 on the request of the lead designer to ensure that the right level of detail was produced by both the building services engineer and the civil and structural engineer at the end of this stage.

- The updates at Stage 3 help to ensure that key aspects of the design will be developed during Stage 3.

RIBA Design Responsibility Matrix incorporating Information Exchanges

Example two: small project

Figure 7.3 Sample from a small project Design Responsibility Matrix

| Aspect of design | | 3. Developed Design | | | 4. Technical Design | | | | 4. Technical Design | | | | Building Contract | |
| | | Design team | | | Design team | | | | Contractor | | | | | |
Uniclass ref	Element	Design Resp.	LOD	Info. Exch.	Design Resp.	LOD	Info. Exch.		Design Resp.	LOD	Info. Exch.		CDP	Note
	Foundations	D2	Out	1:100	D2	F(P)	1:10		N/A	N/A	N/A		No	
	Structure including roof	D2	Out	1:100	D2	F(G)	1:100		C1	F(P)	1:5		Yes	1
	Timber cladding	D1	Out	1:100	D1	F(G)	1:5		C2	F(P)	N/A		No	2
	Render	D1	Out	1:100	D1	P	1:5		C3	F(P)	1:5		Yes	
	Timber windows	D1	Out	1:50	D1	F(G)	1:5		C0	F(P)	1:5		No	3
	Folding aluminium doors	D1	Out	1:50	D1	F(P)	1:5		D1	F(P)	1:5		No	4
	Internal walls	D1	Out	1:50	D1	F(G)	1:5		N/A	N/A	N/A		No	
	Sanitaryware	D1	Out	N/A	D1	F(P)	N/A		N/A	N/A	N/A		No	
	Mechanical services	D3	Out	1:100	D3	F(P)	1:100		N/A	N/A	N/A		No	
	Electrical services	D3	Out	1:100	D3	F(P)	1:100		N/A	N/A	N/A		No	

List of parties with design responsibility

D1 = Unique Ideas Architects
D2 = Green Timber Engineers
D3 = Good Ventilation Designs
C1 = Timber Structures Ltd
C2 = Hardwood Cladding Co.
C3 = White Render Ltd
C0 = Urban Construction Ltdor

Note 1   D1 and D2 to liaise to fix design of visible structural connections between timber trusses prior to tender.

Note 2   D1 to design timber cladding. Contractor to present options for final timber with tender to allow sign-off prior to Building Contract being concluded.

Note 3   D1 to include a number of compliant systems in specification with final selection determined by contractor subject to approval.

Note 4   D1 to select system. Working drawing to be submitted for approval.

Figure 7.3 is not representative of all of the elements of a small project but provides sufficient examples and notes to clarify how the Design Responsibility Matrix should be completed. From this limited worked example of a Design Responsibility Matrix, updated during Stage 4, the following points can be observed:

• The Building Contract has been awarded and the contractor has already confirmed the specialist subcontractors that will be used. The matrix has been updated to include these companies.

• The architect is retaining design responsibility for a number of cladding elements and these elements have not been highlighted for inclusion in the Contractor's Designed Portion of the traditional JCT Building Contract being used. The following points are noted:

— The timber cladding has been specified but the final selection of the timber is left to the contractor, including the visible timber boarding that is specified. To ensure that this is produced to the appropriate quality, the architect has required that this aspect be concluded prior to the Building Contract being finalised. This enables the contractors that are tendering to put forward alternative suggestions but, should these prove unacceptable, for the cost of any alternatives to be factored into the tender appraisal.

— The render element is performance specified and the contractor therefore takes responsibility for this item.

— A number of timber window systems have been sourced and deemed to be acceptable. These are listed in the specification; however, the windows are specified in a generic manner, allowing the contractor to be responsible for the final selection and to put forward alternative proposals in the tender submission if appropriate.

— Due to the technical complexity and the need to finalise supports, etc., the folding aluminium doors have been specified as proprietary products. The schedule reflects the fact that, while the architect retains design responsibility, fabrication drawings are expected to be submitted by the specialist subcontractor for approval.

• In summary, the architect has specified the external cladding aspects in a manner that allows the contractor to provide alternative proposals for a number of items, giving the contractor the possibility of gaining a competitive edge while ensuring that any visible aspects are agreed prior to the Building Contract being awarded.

Figures 7.2 and 7.3 are based on 'analogue' Information Exchanges. The online tool at www.ribaplanofwork.com/toolbox will be updated as further clarification of ('digital') level of detail is achieved. Appendix 1 of the CIC BIM Protocol document contains a Specimen Production and Delivery Table and has a similar purpose to the Design Responsibility Matrix.

What is meant by level of detail?

Although CAD or BIM information is produced 'full size', it is typically issued, or exchanged, as drawings in 'hard' (prints) or 'soft' (electronic) formats, with the level of detail added to the CAD model dictated by the scale of the output (i.e. 1:100, 1:50, 1:5, 1:1, etc.). BIM changes this approach as such outputs are no longer required (although it is likely that 2D 'slices' through a model will continue to be used as contractual documents for some time). The level of detail question therefore progresses from an issue of scale to one of purpose. For example, if the model is being used for design discussions with a client, one level of detail is required in the model, whereas a model being handed over to a specialist subcontractor (for example, to develop the curtain walling) requires a different level of detail. As this transitional subject is in an embryonic state, the Information Exchanges in the Design Responsibility Matrix are conceived in a manner that considers the output scale. Clarity on the appropriate digital level of detail is being developed and will be published in the future.

Schedules of Services

Schedules of Services are required to cover the tasks that cannot be inferred from the agreed Design Responsibility Matrix incorporating Information Exchanges. Schedules of Services:

- define management tasks that have to be undertaken

- allow the project lead or the lead designer to allocate supporting tasks to various roles

- underline the client's objectives

- ensure that project handover duties are properly coordinated and considered, and

- help to align the Building Contract with the professional services contracts.

More specifically, Schedules of Services:

- ensure that any tasks required by the project lead to assist in the management of the project are included in the contracts of the relevant party (for example, particular meetings and their frequency or the need to produce programmes and reports)

- ensure that the tasks required by the lead designer to check that any coordination or integration obligations are adhered to and included in the professional services contracts of the other design team members (for example, when an elemental cost plan is produced)

- ensure that due consideration has been given to any particular tasks that the contractor may require to be carried out in order to comply with internal processes (for example, preparing minutes of meetings with specialist subcontractors or producing Design Programmes in a particular format)

- can be used to contractually underline both the client's requirements for Project Outcomes or Project Objectives and the specific tasks that the client requires to facilitate these at each stage (for example, undertaking design reviews or measuring the developing design against the desired outcomes), and

- are necessary to ensure that any tasks required in Stages 0 and 1 or Stages 6 and 7 are clear (for example, the need to attend a post-occupancy workshop or carrying out a specific Post-occupancy Evaluation).

The appendix provides a multidisciplinary Schedule of Services for each stage of the RIBA Plan of Work 2013. The tasks are derived from the activities stated in the RIBA Plan of Work 2013. These schedules can be expanded as necessary to cover the points set out above using the online tool available at www.ribaplanofwork.com/toolbox.

For those generating bespoke Schedules of Services, some subjects worth considering are listed below.

Handover Strategy

The actions required as a project nears completion and in the post-handover period are covered in the Handover Strategy. This strategy also considers work required in the earlier stages to facilitate these activities. Early agreement of the Handover Strategy is necessary to ensure that the Schedule of Services reflects the required tasks and that the fees of the various parties have been properly considered. The Handover Strategy also frames the tasks that the client wishes to be undertaken during the in-use period. To successfully carry out these tasks may require certain aspects to be undertaken as the design and construction progress or may dictate the way that information is structured and developed for use post occupancy.

Cost Information

Bills of quantities used to be commonplace but are now less frequently used. Pricing schedules, which are typically non-contractual, have replaced bills of quantities on certain projects. These may or may not include quantities. If they do include quantities, the logic is generally to obtain tenders from each contractor based on that information although the successful contractor is typically required to take the cost risk based on 'specification and drawings'. This is typical on design and build contracts and also on certain forms of traditional JCT contracts. Consideration of this risk factor is important for the lead designer, particularly where the procurement route is design and build. In order to assist in the transfer or management of risk, the lead designer may wish to collate a design status schedule, based on information provided by other members of the design team, for inclusion as part of the tender to convey the current status of the design to the contractors tendering for the project.

Collaboration

Collaborative contracts are becoming more commonplace and are considered further in Chapter 10. However, it is important for the project lead, lead designer and construction lead to consider how any collaborative processes might be backed up in any Schedules of Services that are created or to consider the implications that any collaborative contracts, such as PPC2000, NEC3 or JCT's Constructing Excellence contract, may have for the working methods of the project team and include any findings as part of the Communication Strategy within the Project Execution Plan.

Summary

Successful completion of the outputs outlined in this chapter is a fundamental element in the assembly of a collaborative project team. Once the Design Responsibility Matrix incorporating Information Exchanges and Schedules of Services have been completed and all the documents agreed, each member of the project team can be confident that management and design responsibilities have been considered holistically and that all the members of the project team are working towards the same client goals. More importantly, by considering these issues early there is less likelihood of disagreements or disputes arising and the project team is more likely to be focused on the collaborative strategies which are necessary to drive the project forward.

Chapter

WHEN will the project team members undertake their tasks?

What is the purpose of the Project Programme?

What is the aim of a Design Programme?

What purpose does the Construction Programme serve?

How do Design and Construction Programmes differ?

Chapter overview

Programmes have an essential contractual purpose; they also facilitate the day-to-day running of a project and play a crucial role in managing risk. This chapter considers the importance of programmes and differentiates between the different types of programme that might be used on a project.

While professional services contracts have typically contained key milestone dates, historically programmes have not been essential components of construction projects. The crucial cultural shift with the RIBA Plan of Work 2013 is that the Project Programme, and potentially the related Design and Construction Programmes, can become core contractual documents.

What is the purpose of the Project Programme?

The Project Programme sets the strategic periods from briefing to project handover and beyond. It can be made a contractual document for incorporating into both professional services contracts and the Building Contract. It highlights for the design team the periods during which they have to undertake their specific duties (Schedules of Services) and sets out the period for construction and handover. It may identify activities that overlap and create risk and it is therefore essential that the Project Programme is prepared and agreed prior to the parties entering into any contracts.

What is the aim of a Design Programme?

Depending on the nature of the project, the lead designer should prepare a Design Programme, or individual and more detailed programmes for each design stage, to ensure that, in addition to being aware of their own duties or obligations, other parties involved in the design process are aware of what they have to produce and when. Design Programmes should be strategic, since the nature of iterative design, which requires input from clients and third parties whose outputs are not within the control of the project team, makes it difficult to define dates with certainty. It is unlikely that the Project Programme will influence specific design tasks being undertaken at a given stage; however, where stages overlap the lead designer will need to consider any impact on the design process.

The Design Programme is a core management tool for the lead designer and should set out client meeting dates and the timetable for design team meetings as well as key project stage milestones for the design team's reference. The challenge in producing a Design Programme is making it sufficiently detailed to provide guidance to the design team yet not so detailed that the iterative design process is seen to be constantly in delay. To assist with this challenge, the Design Programme must be used in conjunction with other design management tools.

What purpose does the Construction Programme serve?

The Construction Programme is prepared by the contractor and is typically a detailed programme that lists every construction activity that is to occur on site. It focuses on the critical path (activities crucial to the programme, which might cause delay should they fall behind schedule) and allows the contractor to consider buildability and sequencing, health and safety and other construction logistics. It will need to be read in conjunction with method statements, any resource or logistics plans and detailed subcontractor programmes and might be linked to the 3D design model via a 4D model.

Subcontractors will use the Construction Programme to prepare their own detailed programmes and the programme can also be used to monitor progress and to determine whether the proposed completion date is on target.

How do Design and Construction Programmes differ?

Both programmes adhere to the dates set out in the Project Programme; however, Design and Construction Programmes are fundamentally different and have different objectives. Construction Programmes use previous knowledge to estimate finite periods for the construction of each aspect of the building. They can therefore be detailed and will be based on a detailed set of drawings and specifications prepared by the design team and/or specialist subcontractors.

Design Programmes deal with an iterative process that requires inputs from many parties that do not come under the direct control and influence of the project team. Design Programmes therefore need to be more strategic in their nature and aligned to design management tools that monitor the progress of design risks and development.

Further programmes may also be required on a project (for example, off-site fabrication aspects will require their own programme). Procurement programmes are also useful, particularly on a management contract, as each aspect of the building will have different lead-in periods requiring consideration of design, procurement and Construction Programmes in parallel.

Figures 8.1 and 8.2 set out examples of a strategic Project Programme suitable for inclusion in a professional services contract and/or the Building Contract. Figures 8.3 and 8.4 illustrate examples of a Stage 2 and Stage 3 Design Programme, with Figure 8.5 showing an extract from a typical Construction Programme.

Project Programme: large project

Figure 8.1 Project Programme (large project using one-stage design and build procurement)

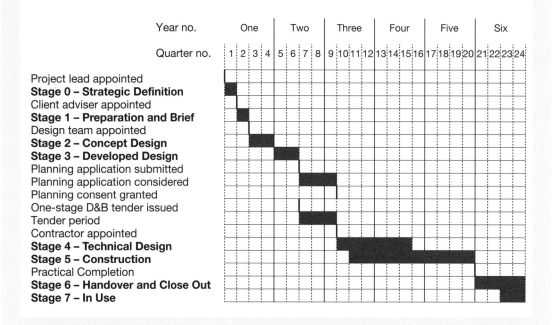

From the limited worked example of the Project Programme illustrated in **Figure 8.1**, the following points can be gleaned:

- A total of three months each have been allocated for Stage 0 and Stage 1.

- A total of six months each have been allocated for Stages 2 and 3.

- The tender is issued to the contractor concurrently with the planning application approval period.

- The design team will be novated to the contractor, with the Stage 4 design work of the design team and the contractor's specialist subcontractors, as defined in the Building Contract, undertaken in parallel over an 18-month period.

- Construction, Stage 5, will take 30 months.

- Stage 6 is shown as one year with limited Stage 7 activities being undertaken during the same timetable.

Note:
(a) By issuing the tender to the contractor at the same time as the planning application is being considered, the project can be progressed with minimal risk to the client. Any planning issues, including agreement of any planning conditions, can be dealt with prior to the award of the Building Contract.
(b) Firm, specific dates can easily be added to the programme once they have been determined in order to bring contractual clarity.

Project Programme: small project

Figure 8.2 Project Programme (small project using traditional procurement)

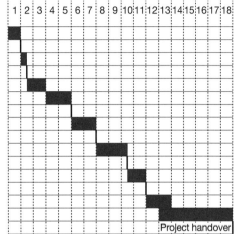

From the limited worked example of the Project Programme shown in **Figure 8.2**, the following points can be gleaned:

- The overall duration of the project from the client deciding to proceed to handover is 18 months.

- City Centre Architects have shown Stage 0 as a brief consultative period, which includes agreement of their fee and appointment. The brief is expanded at Stage 1, along with some Feasibility Studies and the rest of the team are appointed prior to Stage 2 commencing.

- Stage 4 work will not progress until planning consent is granted and is shown as two tranches: the work of the design team prior to tendering and conclusion of the contractor design items after the Building Contract has been awarded.

- Stage 6 is not shown in its entirety as the aim would be to conclude this as soon as possible after project handover and since there are no Stage 7 activities this stage is not shown.

Note:
(a) The overall duration could be reduced by overlapping the design team's Stage 4 with the period required to obtain planning consent. The client would have to accept the risk of doing this (design team fees for abortive or changed work).
(b) Dates are not shown to underline the fact that, in this instance, the programme is indicative. If certain dates were to be contractual (for example, the date for submission of the planning application) these can easily be added.
(c) If the contents of the programme were to be more contractual, client sign-off periods for Stages 3 and 4 would have to be included.

Design Programme: Stage 2 programme

Figure 8.3 Stage 2 programme

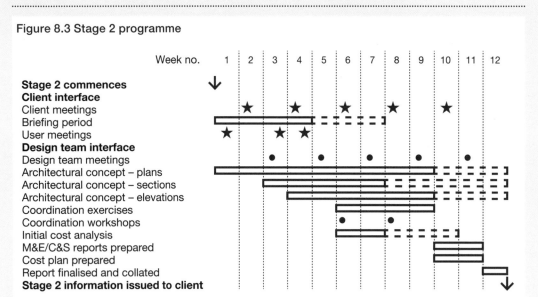

Note: This Design Programme has been copied from **Figure 4.2** of *Leading the Team: An Architect's Guide to Design Management*, where the logic behind the programme and the additional tools required for use in conjunction with the programme are set out in greater detail.

This example of a Stage 2 programme:

- firmly establishes the start of the stage and also the end point, when the project team information will be issued

- focuses on the briefing period, including end user meetings, as well as setting out key client meeting dates

- establishes when the design team will meet, including a number of specific coordination workshops

- sets out when the proposals will be costed by the cost consultant and the reports prepared by the building services and structural engineer will be prepared

- acknowledges that the development of aspects of the general arrangement drawings may extend (dotted line) beyond the programmed date to suit the iterative process (any implications for the rest of the design team's information, if any, would need to be clear in the stage report).

Design Programme: Stage 3 programme

Figure 8.4 Stage 3 programme

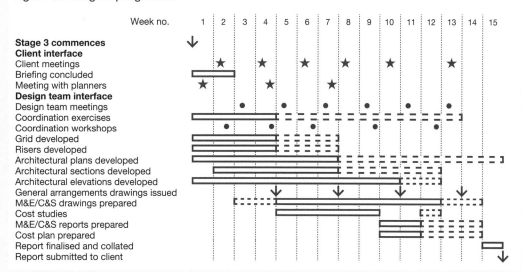

Note: This Design Programme is derived from Figure 4.3 of *Leading the Team: An Architect's Guide to Design Management*, which was based on a Work Stage D programme. It has been extended to include the additional activities necessary to ensure that the Stage 3 design has been coordinated.

This example of a Stage 3 programme:

- firmly establishes the start of the stage and also the end point, when the project team information will be issued

- focuses on how meetings with the planners will be coordinated with client meetings

- places greater emphasis on design team activities; in particular, when core aspects such as risers and grids will be developed

- sets out when the evolving general arrangement drawings will be issued as part of the 'work in progress' of the iterative design process

- contains a two-week contingency period (weeks 13 and 14) for dealing with any planning issues or other 'hot topics' identified as the design develops.

Construction Programme

Figure 8.5 Example of a strategic Construction Programme

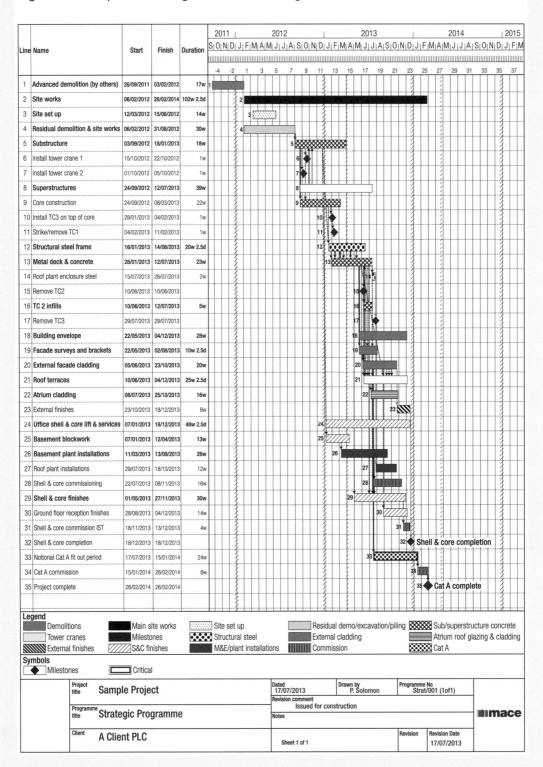

This example of a strategic Construction Programme underlines the differences between a Design Programme and a Construction Programme:

- It has been produced using specialist software that links activities that impact on each other and can be used to identify critical path activities (activities that would directly affect the completion date).

- It is wholly focused on construction and related activities: it is not concerned with some of the issues that a Design Programme addresses, such as client meeting dates.

- It does not consider any statutory consents that may be required or other such matters, including the design work of specialist subcontractors.

- Is used to determine and allocate contractual time periods for the work of subcontractors.

A more detailed construction programme would have the same appearance but it would contain many more detailed construction activities for each 'zone' of the building. Increasingly, programming software is being linked to the BIM model to allow a 3D representation of the construction to be viewed (typically referred to as 4D BIM). This allows health and safety and other logistical issues to be considered in greater detail.

Summary

For programmes to be successful, they must be structured in the most appropriate way. Determining the critical path of a construction project requires different techniques to those used for managing the iterative design process. Successful programming is an essential part of the design and construction processes and transparency of programming is an essential collaborative working tool. The Project Programme is a core contractual document as it sets particular milestones and frames the risks created for each party.

Chapter

HOW will the project team work together?

The value of standards, processes and guidance

What standard protocol documents and guidance exist?

The UK Government

Building Services Research and Information Association (BSRIA)

Royal Institute of British Architects (RIBA)

What should a Project Execution Plan contain?

Chapter overview

Effective processes and protocols are essential if a project is to be successful. The increased use of digital technologies for producing design and other Project Information and the diverse means of communicating that can be adopted on a project require clarity on these subjects at an early stage if communication is be effective. This chapter considers these issues and some of the Common Standards that might be referred to as part of a shift towards 'plug and play' processes.

The scope of and need for project protocols and processes will depend on the size and complexity of a project and the number of organisations involved. However, even on a small project a Project Execution Plan can be a useful document and can be used to corral contact information, the project organogram, communication protocols or other information that may be of use to the client and the project team.

On a BIM project the Project Execution Plan is an essential document. BIM enables faster and more complex design processes. However, these can be only be effective if software, hardware, communication protocols, data exchange formats and other subjects have been considered properly. Put another way, by considering the subjects set out in the second part of this chapter, the collaborative project team will be more effective at Stage 2. Aligned with the WHAT documents, the Project Execution Plan provides the perfect platform for the launch of an effective design period and to assist in the day-to-day running of a project.

Most practices tend to use their internal processes to deal with the HOW aspects. These may be comprehensive and well developed, having evolved over the years. Larger practices are likely to have these processes incorporated within their independently audited Integrated Management System (IMS). BIM requires greater consideration of the project team's processes rather than those of an individual practice or organisation. These can be harnessed more effectively by the project team when Common Standards and working methods are used, particularly for improving communication and minimising compatibility and interoperability issues. At present, because many practices move frequently from project to project, and from one design team and/or project team to another, the challenges associated with agreeing working protocols and methods at the start of a project cannot be underestimated.

Using Common Standards does not negate the work that any practice has put into developing their own processes but it can make working with other practices significantly easier.

This chapter splits into two parts: the first looks at emerging Common Standards that might be considered by a practice or project, with the second part considering what a Project Execution Plan might contain, leaving the judgment on the actual standards and contents to the individual practice or project team.

The value of standards, processes and guidance

When practices focused merely on their own outputs, Common Standards offered fewer benefits. With the advent of BIM this is no longer the case and if a project team is to work together collaboratively Common Standards must be utilised. It is difficult to provide a definitive view on this subject because newly introduced Common Standards have not yet been widely circulated or used. However, in the first part of this chapter some of the existing or emerging new standards and guidance and how they might assist matters are considered.

The difference between Common Standards and legislation

When considering Common Standards it helps to examine the difference between standards and legislation. To be effective, legislation needs to be prescriptive or it would not be possible to ratify compliance with the appropriate legislation. Standards set out best practice or suggested codes of practice in relation to a subject in order to encourage competitors to harness the same systems or protocols (for example, publishing the details of a phone charging socket would mean that competing companies could share information, encouraging them to use the same socket and thereby standardising the use of a product to the benefit of the consumer). From a design perspective, some standards recommend best practice whereas others suggest alternative approaches and care should be taken when using standards in a contractual way, such as inclusion within specifications.

What standard protocol documents and guidance exist?

As outlined above, most practices utilise their own methods for carrying out projects, including CAD/BIM standards. This section considers current Common Standards, their publisher and purpose. One essential consideration is that Common Standards facilitate collaborative working by agreeing certain working methods up front on a project. By selecting Common Standards, disagreements over which practice's protocols are the 'best' can be avoided and, by using Feedback, the Common Standards can be continuously improved.

The UK Government

The UK's Government Construction Strategy, published on 31 May 2011, has acted as a significant catalyst in the drive towards Common Standards and announced the Government's intention to require the use of collaborative 2D BIM (with all project and asset information, documentation and data being in electronic form) on its projects by 2016. The outputs deriving from this initiative have been published by various entities; however, they all serve the same goal and are compatible with the RIBA Plan of Work 2013.

BIM Task Group: www.bimtaskgroup.org

This entity has been established to raise awareness of the UK Government's BIM programme, to ensure that a consistent message is delivered, best practice shared ('work in progress' for a variety of work streams is published) and to allow a feedback route to inform the task group. The website will continue to grow and it is likely that the documents noted below will continue to evolve as exemplar projects are completed.

Digital Plans of Work

In Chapter 7, the value of clear Information Exchanges is set out. A digital Plan of Work expands further on the benefits of clear data requirements and the value that these create. This document in particular aims to clarify how data is defined, tested and used by both the supply chain and the public client. The digital Plans of Work will continue to develop and be accessible via the BIM task group website.

Employer's Information Requirements (EIR)

The Employer's Information Requirements (EIR) template has been developed for inclusion in the tender documents for the procurement of both a design team and the contractor. It requires editing to confirm project-specific requirements, although some elements can be adopted without amendment. Guidance has been written into the template but should be deleted prior to formal issue. EIR are an important element of BIM implementation as they are used to convey to tenderers precisely what BIM models are required and the purposes of those models. In accordance with PAS 1192-2, the design team and constructor should each include an outline BIM Execution Plan (BEP) in their proposals. A compliant BEP will demonstrate how the requirements outlined in the EIR will be met. The content of the EIR covers three areas:

- technical: details of software platforms, definitions of levels of detail, etc.

- management: details of management processes to be adopted in connection with BIM on a project

- commercial: details of BIM model deliverables, timing of data drops and definitions of information purposes.

Plain language questions

BIM creates the potential for more information to be generated on a project. The purpose of the plain language questions is to enable the client to set out those questions that identify the minimum information which must be exchanged at a given stage in order to respond to their queries. This information will increase at each stage. By identifying the client's minimum requirements, the project team would have to justify the need to create additional information beyond this.

COBie-UK-2012

While BSRIA's Design Framework for Building Services 3rd edition (see below) brings clarity regarding the level of drawn detail at each stage, COBie begins to resolve the issue of the data content of a Building Information Model (BIM) at each stage. The game-changing consideration is that COBie detail will be used within a computer aided facilities management (CAFM) system during the life of the building. The incremental development of the data within the BIM model is therefore biased towards in-use functions rather than predicated on its use for construction purposes. The UK Government currently advocates COBie deliverables for its projects.

Government Soft Landings

The Government's own Soft Landings document aims to build on BSRIA's Soft Landings work (see page 101), considering items of particular interest to the UK Government, including operational asset management and greater use of outcome-based specifications set against clear performance criteria.

British Standards Institution (BSI): www.bsigroup.co.uk

BSI produces British Standards under the authority of a Royal Charter. While many practices will use and refer to British Standards during the development of a design, particularly in relation to the specification aspects, very few standards are widely used in relation to design management or processes related to construction. The following standards are being supported by the UK Government's initiatives:

- **BS 1192:2007** *Collaborative production of architectural, engineering and construction information – Code of practice* – a code of practice that sets out the process for the collaborative production of architectural and engineering construction information.

- *Building Information Management. A Standard Framework and Guide to BS 1192* – this book is a guide to BS 1192:2007.

- **PAS 1192-2:2013** *Specification for information management for the capital/ delivery phase of construction projects using building information modelling* – this document builds on the existing code of practice for the collaborative production of architectural, engineering and construction information that is defined within BS 1192:2007. It focuses specifically on the project delivery phase (design and construction) where the majority of graphical data, non-graphical data and documents, known collectively as the Project Information Model (PIM), are created. Its intended audience comprises those responsible for the procurement, design, construction, delivery, operation and maintenance of buildings and infrastructure assets.

- **BS 7000-4:1996** *Design management systems. Guide to managing design in construction* – this standard gives guidance on managing the design process, including sections on design change control, documentation control, validation and verification, design reviews and the design brief. It succinctly summarises the issues that any design management system needs to consider.

The following codes of practice, which are self-explanatory from their titles, set out library objects for various purposes:

- **BS 8541-1:2012** *Library objects for architecture, engineering and construction. Identification and classification. Code of practice.*

- **BS 8541-2:2011** *Library objects for architecture, engineering and construction. Recommended 2D symbols of building elements for use in building information modelling.*

- **BS 8541-3:2012** *Library objects for architecture, engineering and construction. Shape and measurement. Code of practice.*

- **BS 8541-4:2012** *Library objects for architecture, engineering and construction. Attributes for specification and assessment. Code of practice.*

Construction Industry Council (CIC)

The CIC is a representative body for professional bodies, research organisations and other related parties involved in the construction industry. Its broad base allows it to consult and coordinate effectively within the construction industry on a number of emerging standards. Its CIC BIM Forum has been used as a mechanism for disseminating information on some of the publications set out above.

- *CIC BIM Protocol* – the CIC BIM Protocol has been created to allow BIM requirements to be effectively incorporated into professional services contracts and Building Contracts. A number of schedules require to be completed on a project-by-project basis to bring clarity on the level of detail to be produced at each stage and the party responsible for producing this information.

- *Outline Scope of Services for the Role of Information Management* – BIM requires greater clarity regarding data and how it is named, stored and shared, as well as the information that must be exchanged at each stage. This CIC document provides clarity on this new role that helps to facilitate this task.

Building Services Research and Information Association (BSRIA)

BSRIA is a research and consultancy organisation producing best practice guidance in relation to construction with particular focus on building services engineering.

Design Framework for Building Services (3rd edition) – BG 6

This framework has been compiled to identify all of the tasks necessary to develop the building services of a project, allowing each task to be allocated to a specific party. These parties would typically be the building services engineer or the specialist building services subcontractors. In its generic form, the template is blank and has to be completed for inclusion in professional services contracts and the Building Contract. The lead designer must be mindful of any agreements that are made as they may impact on, or conflict with, coordination or integration duties that are included in their professional services contract. The framework also includes drawn examples of the level of detail to which the design should be taken at each project stage, meaning that, from a building services perspective, clarity can be achieved on this subject. BG 6 is currently under review to reflect changes to the stages.

Soft Landings

In the *Guide to Using the RIBA Plan of Work 2013*, Chapter 7 considered the changing nature of project handover and the importance of considering BSRIA's Soft Landings initiative. In addition to considering the duties of the team during handover and the first three years of occupation, this initiative considers the tasks required during the early stages to facilitate a successful handover. In many respects, Soft Landings is a WHAT subject since it considers the Schedules of Services required to deliver the handover (or soft landings) aims. However, as it sets out and considers the working methods required to achieve the soft landings goals, it is also an important HOW document.

The Handover Strategy, as set out in the RIBA Plan of Work 2013, should be used to capture Soft Landings tasks.

Royal Institute of British Architects (RIBA)

The RIBA and its publishing arm, RIBA Enterprises, publish a number of documents and books aimed at bringing clarity on how to run a project and, in particular, the processes which aim to ensuring consistency and how the appropriate level of quality is achieved from project to project.

RIBA QM Toolkit

The RIBA Chartered Practice Manual sets out a tiered approach to Project Quality Plans as follows:

- small practices (up to ten staff in total) are required at least to use the RIBA QM Project Quality Plan, or equivalent, on each project

- medium-sized practices (11 to 49 staff) are required to use the RIBA QM Toolkit (incorporating the RIBA QM Project Quality Plan), or equivalent, on all projects and for office procedures

- large practices (50+ staff) are to have an externally certified BS EN ISO 9001: 2000 Quality Management System in use. This could be based on the RIBA QM Toolkit or an equivalent system.

RIBA Job Book (9th edition)

The *RIBA Job Book* is a long-established and widely recognised standard reference for running construction projects. This edition is based on the RIBA Plan of Work 2013 and current working practices. It embraces themes of collaboration within the project team, better briefing, advances in information technology and BIM, and the continued importance of sustainability, including valuable detail on a range of 'cradle to grave' processes in a building project. It sets out all the actions to be undertaken throughout a project and includes invaluable checklists, notes and practical guidance.

Architect's Handbook of Practice Management (9th edition)

The *Architect's Handbook of Practice Management* is the architect's business management bible. This edition is based on the RIBA Plan of Work 2013 as well as the latest architectural practice management techniques. The book is divided into three parts, focusing in turn on the industry, the practice and the project. The guidance covers education, setting up a practice, professionalism, law, financial management, people management, risk management, QA, IT, marketing strategies and winning clients, alongside innovative topics, such as knowledge management and BIM.

National BIM Library

NBS launched the National BIM Library (www.nationalbimlibrary.com) in March 2012. It is a free-to-use library of standard BIM objects for systems and products, including walls, doors, cladding and roofs.

Leading the Team: An Architect's Guide to Design Management

Project management is a subject that has been considered in some depth. However, there has been limited debate or consideration of the management techniques that assist the development of a design. Design is an iterative process and the lead designer has to employ various techniques and tools in order to manage the development of a design effectively. This publication sets out a number of practical tools that can be harnessed to achieve this goal.

What should a Project Execution Plan contain?

The RIBA Plan of Work 2013 advocates the preparation of a Project Execution Plan during Stage 1 as part of the process of assembling a collaborative project team. The plan could be prepared on a practice or project basis. It may or may not be contractual. It should be accessible to everyone in the project team and there is additional value in new team members undergoing an induction process to ensure that they are aware of the core project procedures.

The purpose of the Plan is simple: to provide information and guidance to the project team in order to facilitate better communication and more collaborative processes. If the Project Execution Plan achieves these goals, it will have been successful. There is no prescriptive list of what a Project Execution Plan should contain but the following might be considered:

- a description of the project (a summary of the brief)

- a project directory

- a company organisation chart

- the Project Roles Table

- the Contractual Tree

- the Design Responsibility Matrix including Information Exchanges

- the Project Programme (the Design Programme(s) might be included or referred to)

- the Technology Strategy (what software, and hardware, will be used)

- the Communication Strategy

- a list of the Common Standards to be adopted

- the CAD/BIM manual, and

- Change Control Procedures.

In some practices, the Plan might be derived from QA processes and may be referred to as the Project Quality Plan or a similar title. The title is, of course, irrelevant. Of primary importance are the contents and ensuring that they are selected to achieve the aims set out above. The contents may vary and be adjusted depending on the client, the scale of the project and the nature of the project team. There may be benefits in certain protocols and processes being referred to or included as appendices rather than being imbedded into the Plan to make the Plan more useable and strategic in nature. Some of the subjects listed above are covered in greater detail below.

Project directory

A directory containing the contact names of every individual involved in a project, their role, and title and contact details is a simple but invaluable tool that can speed up communication. Further clarity can be obtained by issuing a project organisation chart (the Project Roles Table or Contractual Tree could also be used). On larger projects, individual company organisation charts that show internal team structures along with roles and responsibilities can be useful. The directory might be in the form of a document but is now typically part of the information management portal used to facilitate collaborative working.

Communication Strategy

The Communication Strategy should consider all aspects of communication on a project. For example:

- Meetings
  - What types of meetings are required; how often and where will they be held?
  - If meetings are to be held remotely, does the Technology Strategy set out how this will occur?
  - Who will chair and minute the meetings?

- Queries
  - How will queries be raised and resolved?
  - How can they be logged for future reference?
  - How can they be monitored to ensure that no backlogs occur and to check the accuracy of responses?

- Data exchange formats and transfer mechanisms
  - How will information be transferred between members of the project team?
  - What file formats will be used for transferring information?
  - What is the means of transferring information (email/extranet/FTP site/ file-sharing software, etc.)? See the section on the Technology Strategy below.

Technology Strategy

Although the UK Government is advocating the use of Level 2 BIM on all public sector projects by 2016, many designers will continue to use traditional tools well into the future. To accommodate these situations, the Technology Strategy may stipulate that no technology is to be used (the design may use freehand sketches, for example). However, it will normally set out the software and hardware that the project team will utilise on a project.

Software

The software selected can have a significant effect on a project. It is less likely to have an impact where specialist software is used by a single party (an energy or structural analysis package, for example) but the core modelling platform can be a crucial issue since, despite the move towards interchangeable outputs, problems can be encountered when transferring from one file format output to another. In some instances, additional software or processes may be required to undertake tasks, such as clash detection where the team is using different software and, in extreme circumstances, it may not be possible for one project team member to use certain outputs generated by others. Furthermore, different versions of the same software packages can be incompatible and present additional problems. Asking each party to state in the Technology Strategy the software, and its version, to be used allows any potential issues to be dealt with during Stage 1. In some instances, the client may impose requirements to ensure that all the members of the project team are working on the same software platforms and versions. This gives the client the confidence that no fee or process issues will arise from this aspect of the project.

Hardware

Hardware is not likely to be a project issue as most members of the project team will use computers suitable for running their specific software packages. However, certain hardware may be required to accommodate the Communication Strategy (video conferencing equipment, for example) and it is therefore beneficial for all members of the team to set out the hardware that they are likely to be using on a project so that any potential issues related to proposed software can be investigated and resolved.

Training

Any training requirements should be highlighted in the Technology Strategy. For example, a new portal might be implemented for the collaborative exchange and storage of information, requiring training for all members of the project team.

The exchange formats to be issued for different elements of information and the means of exchanging them are also crucial technology issues. This will inevitably involve a degree of overlap as these issues are also covered in the Communication Strategy, as set out above.

CAD/BIM manual

The CAD/BIM manual should cover the proposed working methods of any party in the project team producing CAD and/or BIM information. The CAD/BIM manual might cover the following aspects:

- Coordinate strategy – this would include the origin to be used for all of the models as well as the means of transferring any grids to any permanent or temporary benchmarks on site.

- Standards – the standards that the project team will adhere to. Adherence to standards may require individual parties to alter their in-house CAD/BIM manuals.

- Coordination – the process to be used by the lead designer for the coordination of BIM models must be considered and also, where appropriate, how clash detection software will be used to check that coordination exercises are complete. In some instances clashes may be managed rather than resolved (for example, it may be deemed unnecessary to punch holes in the floor assembly where floor boxes are placed).

- Naming conventions, including zone strategies – the project-wide strategy for naming drawings and files in order to assist searching and sourcing of the files on a day-to-day basis. On larger projects the building may need to be broken down into zones. The zonal strategy should be agreed by all members of the project team before it is implemented.

The CAD/BIM manual will have overlaps with the Technology and Communication Strategies and other aspects of the Project Execution Plan. Ultimately, the location of the requisite information is not important. It is more important that each subject has been considered and a strategy prepared, agreed and included somewhere in the Plan.

Change Control Procedures

Establishing robust Change Control Procedures is an essential requirement of any project. The RIBA Plan of Work 2013 advocates that these be established during Stage 2 (although some clients may do this from the outset) for implementation during Stage 3. This, of course, assumes that no major changes to the brief occur during Stage 2, in which case any fee issues would need to be addressed separately. The rationale for being more robust from the start of Stage 3 is that all of the design team members will be developing the Concept Design signed off by the client at the end of Stage 2 so, from that stage onwards, the amount of information increases exponentially (see Figure 1.1 on page 6). In some situations there is a fine line between change and design development. The rule is simple: if the Concept Design changes then change control is required. If details are developed that are affordable within the cost plan, this is design development. At the end of the day, a degree of common sense is required.

The same applies to any processes that are developed. They must be robust enough to record the key facts and allow the client to sign off change, yet they must be sufficiently streamlined not to impede or impact design or construction progress by generating mountains of paperwork.

Collaborative process

Every project team will have its own views on the best ways of undertaking the 'softer' aspects of collaboration, as well as on the use of standards and day-to-day tools that help to facilitate this process. It is therefore worth setting these out in a section of the Project Execution Plan to further emphasise the collaborative approach being used and help to ensure that each member of the team buys into the agreed strategy.

Reviews and quality control

The lead designer will need a process for commenting on information as it progresses and the project lead and others, including the client, may have to comment, or approve, information as it is produced. Some parties will have quality assurance procedures to adhere to. The processes and timescales for these activities have to be considered. Certain parties may also have internal processes that must be adhered to and may wish the Design Programme to reflect these periods. Where a common software package is to be harnessed to provide comments it should be stated in the Technology Strategy.

Confidentiality and security

The professional services contracts or Building Contracts may not be accessible to all members of the project team. It is therefore worthwhile to state any required confidentiality or other security measures or processes in the Project Execution Plan to underline the importance of this subject and, more importantly, to ensure that any requirements are transparent and obvious to every project team member.

The RIBA Plan of Work 2013 advocates preparation of the Project Execution Plan during Stage 1 because consideration of the topics contained in the Project Execution Plan is an essential part of properly building a successful and collaborative project team. Furthermore, the document can be used for recording core decisions and agreements. More importantly, consideration of the topics contained in the Project Execution Plan may flag fee or project and design management issues. These are best addressed and resolved before Stage 2 commences.

Finally, depending on circumstances, the Project Execution Plan may be contractual or non-contractual in its nature and it should be developed accordingly.

Summary

The concept of Common Standards failed to gain traction in recent years. BIM requires greater consideration of these to enable parties to move seamlessly from one project to the next. The Project Execution Plan is an essential tool for recording agreements on how the project team will communicate, exchange information and manage the project on a day-to-day basis and for setting the collaborative techniques that will be used by the project team.

Chapter

10

Contracts for the collaborative project team

Professional services contracts

Building Contracts

Collaborative project team contracts

Chapter overview

Once the WHY, WHO, WHAT, WHEN and HOW aspects have been considered, they need to be collated with other documents to form professional services contracts (appointments) and/or Building Contracts. This chapter considers the commonly used contracts and some of the additional factors that must be taken into account if these various contracts are to be compatible on a particular project.

As well as establishing methods for dealing with day-to-day issues on a project, the steps set out in Chapters 6 to 9 produce documents suitable for binding into contractual documents. In summary, at the end of the WHY, WHO, WHAT, WHEN and HOW stages, the following aspects will have been considered and agreed:

- the project brief

- the required project roles

- the timing of contractor involvement

- the allocation of roles to specific parties (Project Roles Table)

- contractual relationships (Contractual Tree)

- a Design Responsibility Matrix incorporating Information Exchanges, Multidisciplinary Schedules of Services and the fees associated with these documents

- the Project Programme and corresponding Design and Construction Programmes, and

- project protocols, as set out in the Project Execution Plan.

It is possible for the preparation of the documents to have occurred in a collaborative manner (using a workshop, for example), and it is also feasible that, as each step has progressed, members of the project team will have been incrementally appointed and able to contribute to the appointment of other members of the team. Whatever the facts of the specific case, the steps set out in Chapters 6 to 9 have been conceived to ensure that the appointment of the various parties in the project team is as straightforward as possible.

In this chapter, the interface of the completed tools with commonly available professional services contracts and Building Contracts is considered. The pros and cons of collaborative contracts that seek to bind the client, design team and contractor together in a more cohesive way are also set out.

In many circumstances, the forms of professional services contract and Building Contract to be used on a project or by a client or practice will already have been determined.

Professional services contracts

Broadly speaking, design team members will be appointed using professional services contracts regardless of the Contractual Tree or the procurement method used to select them. These contracts, between the client and the consultant, are also frequently referred to as 'agreements' or 'appointments'. In some instances, another design team member or the contractor will be the client.

There are two ways to appoint designers: using an 'off the shelf' document (also known as 'standard form appointments') or by preparing a bespoke appointment. The former are generally prepared by a particular industry body and contain standard clauses in relation to matters such as copyright, confidentiality, etc. and generic clauses in relation to fees and programme for completion on each specific project. These standard form appointments have been tried and tested in the industry and have been assembled with the assistance of legal advisers.

Bespoke professional services contracts (appointments) are likely to contain the same project-specific information but, as they are typically prepared by a client's legal team, they are likely to have more onerous terms in relation to matters such as copyright, confidentiality, etc. Consultation carried out by the RIBA in relation to the development of the RIBA Plan of Work 2013 revealed that many architects encounter bespoke appointments on a regular basis. It is important for consultants to seek advice from their legal advisers and professional indemnity (PI) insurers before agreeing to such appointments although they must also consider their own views in relation to fee, programme or Schedule of Services issues. *Law in Practice: The RIBA Legal Handbook* provides a useful insight into the types of clauses likely to be encountered in a bespoke or standard form contract.

Further complications arise for those undertaking the lead designer role or other roles that require the management of parties that they do not directly employ. For those undertaking the project lead or lead designer role it is essential that they contribute to, or have sight of and agree to, the Design Responsibility Matrix incorporating Information Exchanges and Schedule of Services documents for the other members of the project team. The holistic nature of the RIBA Plan of Work 2013, its alignment to RIBA Appointments and the tools set out in this book assist in this task.

Any professional services contract will also require consideration of certain aspects, such as the level of PI insurance cover or dispute resolution methods. These considerations do not alter the need to use the tools set out in this publication and these aspects are not considered in this publication. The project fee must also be included in any professional services contract. This is likely to be influenced by the outputs set out in this publication.

Subconsultant agreements, collateral warranties and novation agreements may also be required to 'join the dots' between other parties in the project team or to connect them to third parties with a vested interest in a project (a tenant, for example). Information on these contractual documents is also contained in *The RIBA Legal Handbook*.

As a reminder, the 'kit of parts' that has been set out in this publication can be used with the RIBA, or other, forms of appointment, and consists of the outputs from the process that builds a project team, as illustrated in **Figure 10.1**.

One further complication is that one consultant may need to appoint another (see Contractual Tree examples on pages 64 and 66). This can be done with the same professional services contracts, but an alternative is to use a subconsultant agreement, such as the version available in the RIBA suite of appointment documents. Either way, the crucial point is that the requirements set out in the contract with the subconsultant should be 'back-to-back' with the contract put in place with the client.

Figure 10.1 Stage 1 outputs for inclusion in contracts

Strategic Brief and Initial Project Brief **Project Budget**	**WHY**
Project Roles Table **Contractual Tree**	**WHO**
Schedules of Services **Design Responsibility Matrix** **Information Exchanges**	**WHAT**
Project Design and Construction **Programmes**	**WHEN**
Project Execution Plan including Technology and Communication Strategies	**HOW**

'Off-the-shelf' professional services contracts

Royal Institute of British Architects (RIBA): www.ribabookshops.com
RIBA Enterprises produces a number of professional services contracts (appointments) on behalf of the RIBA for use by architects or other consultants. The suite also includes a subconsultant contract allowing the back-to-back appointment of one consultant by another. The suite has been prepared for use on large and small projects and to accommodate both domestic and non-domestic clients. While those using the RIBA documents will be familiar with the various forms of Building Contract in existence, care is required to ensure that the

Building Contract is aligned with the completed professional services contracts. For example, ensuring that the consultant appointments (professional services contracts) are aligned to any contractor design responsibility included in the Building Contract. The suite comprises:

- RIBA Concise Conditions of Appointment for an Architect – this suite of documents is intended for use on small non-domestic projects

- RIBA Conditions of Appointment for an Architect for a Domestic Project – as the title suggests, this suite is intended for use on residential projects

- RIBA Standard Conditions of Appointment for an Architect – for use on all other projects of any size. This appointment document can be used by the client in conjunction with the Standard Conditions of Appointment for a Consultant, allowing the client to appoint other consultants under the same terms as the architect.

NEC (formerly the New Engineering Contract): www.neccontract.com
The NEC Professional Services Contract (PSC) is intended for use in the appointment of any member of the project or design team providing professional services and is now the form of contract used on the majority of public sector projects. As well as including clauses on matters typically covered in other standard forms (such as indemnity, insurance and liability, termination, dispute resolution and payment) the NEC PSC includes clauses on other important subjects, such as early warnings, the programme, the risk register, communications and compensation events. The contract relies on mutual trust and cooperation and the inclusion of these subjects aims to make the contract more collaborative. The PSC is aligned with the NEC3 Building Contract to ensure that the contractor is appointed in the same collaborative manner as the rest of the project team.

Construction Industry Council (CIC): www.cicshop.co.uk
The CIC Consultants' Contract package consists of the CIC Conditions (2nd edition) and the CIC Scope of Services. The Conditions have been developed for use by experienced clients and consultants working on major building projects and can be used by either development clients or contractor clients for the appointment of any member of the design team. A number of supporting documents work in conjunction with the package, including a warranty and novation agreement. The CIC Scope of Services aims to provide clarity regarding the tasks to be undertaken by each project role and also contains a template

for allocating design responsibility. It has been developed for use with the CIC Conditions and other forms of contract but has not been widely adopted.

Joint Contracts Tribunal (JCT): www.jctltd.co.uk
While the JCT's primary focus is the development of their comprehensive suite of Building Contracts, they also produce a consultancy agreement specifically designed for use by public sector clients. This professional services agreement can be used for the appointment of any member of the design team and is suitable for use with the majority of JCT Building Contracts.

FIDIC Client/Consultant Model Services Agreement (4th edition)
This is an international consultant agreement aligned to the FIDIC Building Contracts. This agreement is used predominately on large international engineering and building projects. This appointment works in a similar manner to NEC3 with certain clauses providing project-specific data.

GC/Works (formerly, Government Conditions)
The GC/Works suite of contracts contains the General Conditions for the Appointment of Consultants, which can be used on a single project, and a separate version for use on frameworks. The contracts are aligned to the building GC/Works Building Contracts. They were created primarily for government projects and are still available, although they are no longer being updated. The majority of government contracts now adopt the NEC3 outlined above.

ACA SFA 2012: ACA Standard Form of Agreement for the Appointment of an Architect
This contract closely follows its predecessor SFA/99. It is suitable for commercial and consumer projects and includes model letters for each kind of project to assist architects and their clients to come to a fair agreement on contract terms.

Building Contracts

The Building Contract between the client and the contractor is a pivotal and essential component of any project, primarily because this contract will relate to the majority of the Project Budget and is likely to deal with the most significant risks.

Building Contracts exist in a number of standard forms and these are summarised below. Such contracts set out how the parties will deal with matters such as payments, variations, insurances, preliminaries and penalties for late delivery. This guidance document does not consider these issues or how to select the most appropriate form of Building Contract. However, such guidance can be obtained in *Which Contract?* published by RIBA Enterprises.

It is important to consider the interface between the professional services contracts and the Building Contract. If this task is properly addressed, the Building Contract should align with the design team's professional services contracts. One method of ensuring contract compatibility is to use professional services contracts and a Building Contract that have been produced by the same publisher. This, however, is not always possible as many publishers produce only professional services contracts and not Building Contracts, or vice versa. Due to the diverse views on the best contracts to use, it is still therefore essential to understand why it is important to ensure that both forms of contract are aligned.

As a reminder, the contractor may have design responsibilities either for some or all aspects of the design, although this design work will typically be undertaken by members of the design team and/or specialist subcontractors.

'Off-the-shelf' Building Contracts

Building Contracts are provided by a number of publishing organisations. The most commonly used are listed below. As well as publishing Building Contracts, some of these organisations produce additional contractual and supporting documentation such as subcontracts, forms of tender, warranties, performance and retention bonds, parent company guarantees and guidance notes. Furthermore, some publishers also publish professional services contracts (see the previous section). The use of Building Contracts that are specifically aligned with professional services contracts (or vice versa) is one method of ensuring that all members of the project team have been appointed in a holistic way. However, it must be remembered that all of these contracts are 'light' on the outputs covered in Chapters 6 to 9 (i.e. they do not deal specifically with them) and this should be considered when preparing the various contracts.

JCT (Joint Contracts Tribunal): www.jctltd.co.uk

JCT Building Contracts are the most frequently used contracts in the UK construction industry. A diverse set of contracts is available for use with different procurement routes: for example, traditional, design and build and management contracting. Simpler versions are available for use on smaller projects and, more significantly, options are available to allow the inclusion (or exclusion) of Performance Specified Work and also to allow contracts to be entered into with or without quantities. Commonly used contracts include:

- JCT Minor Works Building Contract 2011 (MW)
- JCT Standard Building Subcontract with Subcontractor's Design Agreement 2011 (SBCSub/D/A)
- JCT Design and Build Contract 2011 (DB)
- JCT Management Building Contract 2011 (MC)
- JCT Construction Management Appointment 2011 (CM/A)
- JCT Intermediate Building Contract 2011 (IC)
- JCT Homeowner/Occupier Agreement (HO).

NEC (formerly New Engineering Contract): www.neccontract.com

NEC is a family of standard contracts developed using clear and simple language with the aim of fostering collaborative working relations between the two contracting parties. The contracts are suitable for use on the majority of projects and in a range of project scenarios. The third edition (commonly referred to as NEC3) of the NEC Engineering and Construction Contract is the current form of contract and is aligned with the NEC Professional Services Contract. NEC contracts are suitable for procuring a diverse range of projects, spanning major framework projects through to minor works and for the purchasing of supplies and goods. The Construction Clients' Group Board (formerly the Public Sector Construction Clients' Forum) endorses the NEC3 contracts for use by public sector organisations when procuring construction. The aim is to standardise the use of this comprehensive suite of contracts in order to help deliver efficiencies across the public sector and promote behaviours which align with the principles of Achieving Excellence in Construction.

Chartered Institute of Building (CIOB): www.ciob.org

The CIOB Contract for Complex Projects was launched in May 2013 and is a new form of contract devised for use on larger projects for use by experienced clients. It uses a 'plain English' approach and it is anticipated that it will be favoured internationally, where FIDIC is seen as overcomplicated, and in the UK for those who choose not to use JCT contracts. With the NEC3 favoured by the public sector and JCT delivering numerous options, it is difficult to predict who might use this contract. Furthermore, it is not aligned with any professional services contracts.

International Federation of Consulting Engineers (FIDIC): http://fidic.org

FIDIC developed the Conditions of Contract First Edition: Red Book to allow international contracting standards to be introduced throughout the world, particularly in locations where standard forms of contract did not exist or were in a format unsuitable for use by international contractors and consultants, and to enable engineers to consistently deliver projects. This agreement is predominately used on large international engineering and building projects.

GC/Works (formerly, Government Conditions)

This suite of standard Government conditions of contract (GC Works) was created primarily for government projects and they are still available although they are no longer being updated. The majority of Government contracts now adopt the NEC3 outlined above.

Collaborative project team contracts

Another means by which a client can contract with the design team and the contractor is to utilise a partnering or collaborative contract. The two commonly used contracts that achieve this, along with their pros and cons, are set out below. These contracts are either constructed in a manner that enables them to be used to appoint any member of the project team or devised as multi-party contracts in which all the core members of the project team sign up to the same terms and conditions.

Collaborative working and problem-solving methods are a core component of such contracts and they may also include means of measuring performance or setting out the client's goals and objectives. Some clients have traditionally used standard forms of contract and asked project team members to sign a non-binding collaborative 'contract'. Collaborative contracts take this principle a stage further with the commitments made binding.

'Off-the-shelf' collaborative project team contracts

Joint Contracts Tribunal (JCT): www.jctltd.co.uk

The JCT Constructing Excellence contract (JCT/CE) was launched in 2007 and is derived from the 'collaborative contract' originally published in 2003 by BE (a joint venture between the Reading Construction Forum and the Design and Build Foundation and now part of Constructing Excellence). It is suitable for the procurement of construction works and/or for the provision of professional services and where participants wish to engender collaborative and integrated working practices. It is the JCT's first 'partnering' contract and it introduces the concept of an 'overriding principle' of collaboration under which the parties must support collaborative behaviour and confront any practice which is 'anti-collaborative'. The contract also introduces the concept of a project team.

The project team guides the successful delivery of the project through its design and construction phases and to achieve this objective they are required to 'meet regularly'. The project team members are encouraged to prepare and adopt a project protocol that sets out the team's aims and objectives with regard to the delivery of the project and the development of their working relationships. Other tools include the preparation of a risk register and a risk allocation schedule.

In 2009, the Office of Government Commerce (OGC) agreed to endorse the use of this contract as part of their Achieving Excellence in Construction initiative.

ACA Standard Form of Contract for Project Partnering PPC2000: Amended 2008

The ACA's PPC2000 brings together the client, design team and contractor under a single multi-party contract. The core members of the project team sign the agreement and, as further members join the project team, they sign a Joining Agreement, with specialist subcontractors signing a back-to-back SPC2000 specialist contract for project partnering. The multi-party contract replaces the many bilateral contracts that the client would normally sign, and avoids the separate partnering agreement sometimes bolted on to the traditional contract forms.

The contract includes incentivisation clauses (for example, shared savings or rewards linked to early delivery of the project), aimed at changing traditional adversarial attitudes, and a risk register along with key performance indicators (KPIs) and targets can be incorporated into the contract. The partnering and project timetable is a core part of the contract, and design and process (HOW) aspects are also included.

118

Summary

The steps and tools presented in this publication have been set out in a manner that allows the best possible project team to be created, in line with the client's specific objectives. The Project Outputs should be set out at Stage 1, regardless of project size, and they can accompany professional services contracts and Building Contracts as they are produced. The project team can then progress to Stage 2 confident that many of the subjects that typically give rise to problems on a project have already been dealt with and secure in the knowledge that they have the tools to facilitate a collaborative project. In this chapter, the purpose of professional services contracts and Building Contracts has been set out, along with the standard forms that are commonly available for both. This publication advocates two approaches:

1 Use of a RIBA or CIC professional services contract with the appropriate JCT contract – this method has been in use for a number of years, although many clients prefer to use a bespoke professional services agreement and also modify the selected JCT contract.

2 The use of the NEC3 Professional Services Contract with an NEC3 Building Contract. This route is increasingly being used on public sector contracts and encourages a collaborative approach.

The use of a FIDIC professional services contract with a FIDIC Building Contract on international projects where the client is unfamiliar with RIBA, CIC, JCT and NEC documents would also be supported.

While the RIBA fully endorses the use of collaborative contracts, this publication proposes that, by properly defining the project team and determining WHO does WHAT, WHEN and HOW, standard forms of contract are suitable for collaborative projects, since the process of using the tools set out in this publication engenders a collaborative approach and ensures that all members of the project team are aware of their obligations. More importantly, emphasis can be placed on harnessing the soft skills required to make a collaborative project team work efficiently, confident that, in the event of a dispute arising, the requisite documents are in place for reference.

Appendix

Multidisciplinary Schedules of Services

The multidisciplinary Schedules of Services set out on the following pages have been developed to align with the RIBA Plan of Work 2013 by allocating each of the tasks set out in the Plan to one of the core roles for each stage of a project. Where a particular task requires one role to support another, the requisite tasks have also been identified.

While this 'hardcopy' version of the Schedules of Services can be utilised, it has not been designed to be definitive and it is recommended that the version at www.ribaplanofwork.com/toolbox, which is free to download, is used. The online version:

- includes activities specific to procurement and tendering, which can be added at the appropriate stage depending on the chosen procurement route (see below)

- will be updated in line with the Feedback received

- allows tasks to be moved from one role to another where this is deemed relevant (a feature which may be of particular interest to those developing practice-specific Schedules of Services)

- allows additional project roles and the requisite tasks to be added.

While the Schedules of Services focus on the core management tasks that are required, the inclusion of further, more detailed management tasks may also be beneficial on certain projects. For example:

- specific reporting requirements

- particular expectations for attendance at meetings

- precise requirements for the review of information.

These types of task might feasibly be included in a management responsibility matrix incorporated within the Design Responsibility Matrix. In any event, the completed Schedules of Services and Design Responsibility Matrix incorporating Information Exchanges should provide a comprehensive set of tasks for a multidisciplinary team, moulded to suit the particular requirements of a practice or project.

Specific Stage 7 duties have not been included. It is currently envisaged that they would be incorporated within separate professional services contracts or operational contracts.

The procurement tasks that might be added in Stages 1 to 4, depending on the procurement route, include:

- as part of the process of assembling the project team, agreeing the procurement route with the client and determining the form of Building Contract to be used

- preparing a list of potential contractors and agreeing the shortlist with the client

- collating information gathered by the project team and assembling the Employer's Requirements

- collating and issuing information for tender purposes

- assessing contractors' tenders, preparing reports and making recommendations to the client

- reviewing the Contractor's Proposals with the project team and agreeing the final set of documents for incorporation into the Building Contract.

The provision of specific documents to support the RIBA Plan of Work is new and it is anticipated that they will be fine tuned on a regular basis in response to Feedback.

Stage 0

Strategic Definition

Project role		Tasks to be undertaken
All roles	☐	
Client and/or client adviser	☐	• Provide Business Case and other core project requirements and contribute to development of Strategic Brief as required
Project lead	☐ ☐ ☐ ☐	• Collate comments and facilitate workshops to discuss Business Case and develop Strategic Brief with project team members • Discuss initial considerations for assembling the project team • Establish Project Programme • Collate Feedback from previous projects
Lead designer	☐ ☐ ☐	• Contribute to preparation of Strategic Brief • Comment on Project Programme • Provide Feedback from previous projects
Architect	☐ ☐ ☐	• Contribute to preparation of Strategic Brief • Discuss project with appropriate planning authority • Provide Feedback from previous projects
Building services engineer	☐	• Contribute to preparation of Strategic Brief
Civil and structural engineer	☐	• Contribute to preparation of Strategic Brief
Cost consultant	☐	• Provide Cost Information, including benchmarking, as part of Strategic Brief
Construction lead		N/A
Contract administrator		N/A
Health and safety adviser	☐	
All additional project roles	☐	• Contribute to preparation of Strategic Brief

Where it is appropriate to allocate an additional task(s) to a specific role(s) or to move a task to a different role, the template available at www.ribaplanofwork.com/toolbox can be used to add these tasks.

Stage 1

Preparation and Brief

Project role		Tasks to be undertaken
All roles	☐	• Provide information for and contribute to contents of Project Execution Plan as required
Client and/or client adviser	☐	• Contribute to development of Initial Project Brief, including Project Objectives, Quality Objectives, Project Outcomes, Sustainability Aspirations, Project Budget and other parameters or constraints
Project lead	☐ ☐ ☐ ☐ ☐ ☐	• Develop Initial Project Brief with project team, including Project Objectives, Quality Objectives, Project Outcomes, Sustainability Aspirations, Project Budget and other parameters or constraints • Collate comments and facilitate workshops as required to develop Initial Project Brief • Prepare Project Roles Table and Contractual Tree and continue to assemble project team and appoint team members • Prepare Schedule of Services and develop Design Responsibility Matrix incorporating Information Exchanges in collaboration with lead designer • Review Project Programme and Feasibility Studies, Prepare Handover Strategy, Risk Assessments and Project Execution Plan • Monitor and review progress and performance of project team
Lead designer	☐ ☐ ☐ ☐ ☐	• Where required, contribution to preparation of Initial Project Brief • Assist in assembling project team • Contribute to preparation of Handover Strategy and Risk Assessments • Comment on Project Programme • Monitor and review progress and performance of design team
Architect	☐ ☐ ☐ ☐	• Contribute to preparation of Initial Project Brief • Discuss project with appropriate planning authority • Undertake Feasibility Studies • Prepare Site Information report
Building services engineer	☐ ☐	• Assist in preparation of Initial Project Brief • Contribute to Site Information report
Civil and structural engineer	☐ ☐	• Assist in preparation of Initial Project Brief • Contribute to Site Information report
Cost consultant	☐ ☐	• Assist in preparation of Initial Project Brief • Prepare Project Budget in consultation with client
Construction lead		N/A
Contract administrator		N/A
Health and safety adviser	☐	
All additional project roles	☐	• Where required, contribute to preparation of Initial Project Brief

Where it is appropriate to allocate an additional task(s) to a specific role(s) or to move a task to a different role, the template available at www.ribaplanofwork.com/toolbox can be used to add these tasks.

Stage 2

Concept Design

Project role	Tasks to be undertaken
All roles	☐ • Contribute to Health and Safety Strategy as required ☐ • Provide information for and contribute to contents of Project Execution Plan as required ☐ • Contribute to development of Final Project Brief
Client and/or client adviser	☐ • Comment on Concept Design proposals as they progress ☐ • Sign off Concept Design and Final Brief ☐ • Comment on Project Strategies as requested
Project lead	☐ • Monitor progress of Concept Design ☐ • Collate and agree changes to initial Project Brief and issue Final Project Brief ☐ • Review Handover Strategy and Risk Assesments with project team ☐ • Review and update Project Execution Plan ☐ • Review Project Programme and agree any changes with project team ☐ • Comment on stage Design Programme and Cost Information ☐ • Monitor and review progress and performance of project team
Lead designer	☐ • Comment on design proposals and Project Strategies of design team members ☐ • Prepare Sustainability Strategy and Maintenance and Operational Strategy with inputs from project team as required ☐ • Prepare stage Design Programme with input from other design team members ☐ • Comment on Cost Information ☐ • Monitor and review progress and performance of design team
Architect	☐ • Prepare architectural Concept Design in accordance with the Initial Project Brief, Design Responsibility Matrix incorporating Information Exchanges and Design Programme ☐ • Liaise with planning authorities as required ☐ • Submit planning application (recommended at Stage 3) ☐ • Undertake third party consultations and any Research and Development aspects as required ☐ • Assist lead designer with preparation of stage Design Programme ☐ • Provide information for preparation of Cost Information and Project Strategies
Building services engineer	☐ • Prepare Concept Design for building services design in accordance with the Initial Project Brief, Design Responsibility Matrix incorporating Information Exchanges and Design Programme ☐ • Undertake third party consultations as required and any Research and Development aspects ☐ • Assist lead designer with preparation of stage Design Programme ☐ • Provide information for preparation of Cost Information and Project Strategies
Civil and structural engineer	☐ • Prepare Concept Design for structural design in accordance with the Initial Project Brief, Design Responsibility Matrix incorporating Information Exchanges and Design Programme ☐ • Undertake third party consultations as required and any Research and Development aspects ☐ • Assist lead designer with preparation of stage Design Programme ☐ • Provide information for preparation of Cost Information and Project Strategies
Cost consultant	☐ • Prepare preliminary Cost Information ☐ • Assist lead designer with preparation of stage Design Programme
Construction lead	☐ • Prepare Construction Strategy
Contract administrator	N/A
Health and safety adviser	☐ • Develop Health and Safety Strategy, including statutory requirements
All additional project roles	☐ • Liaise with project lead and lead designer as required ☐ • Provide information as set out in the Design Responsibility Matrix incorporating Information Exchanges in accordance with Design Programme

Stage 3

Developed Design

Project role		Tasks to be undertaken
All roles	☐ ☐	• Contribute to Health and Safety Strategy as required • Provide information for and contribute to contents of Project Execution Plan as required
Client and/or client adviser	☐ ☐ ☐	• Comment on Developed Design proposals as they progress • Sign off Developed Design • Comment on updated Project Strategies as requested
Project lead	☐ ☐ ☐ ☐ ☐ ☐ ☐	• Monitor progress of developing design • Review updated Handover Strategy and Risk Assesments with project team • Review and update Project Execution Plan • Review Project Programme and agree any changes with project team • Comment on stage Design Programme and Cost Information • Manage change control progress • Monitor and review progress and performance of project team
Lead designer	☐ ☐ ☐ ☐ ☐	• Coordinate and comment on design proposals and Project Strategies as they progress • Update Sustainability Strategy and Maintenance and Operational Strategy with input from project team as required • Prepare stage Design Programme in conjunction with other design team members • Comment on Cost Information • Monitor and review progress and performance of design team
Architect	☐ ☐ ☐ ☐ ☐ ☐	• Prepare architectural Developed Design in accordance with the Design Responsibility Matrix incorporating Information Exchanges, Design Programme and coordination comments from lead designer • Liaise with planning authorities as required • Submit planning application • Undertake third party consultations as required and conclude any Research and Development aspects • Assist lead designer with preparation of stage Design Programme • Provide information for updated Cost Information and Project Strategies
Building services engineer	☐ ☐ ☐ ☐	• Prepare building services Developed Design in accordance with the Design Resonsibility Matrix incorporating Information Exchanges, Design Programme and coordination comments from lead designer • Undertake third party consultations and any Research and Development aspects as required • Assist lead designer with preparation of stage Design Programme • Provide information for preparation of Cost Information and Project Strategies
Civil and structural engineer	☐ ☐ ☐ ☐	• Prepare coordinated and updated proposals for structural design in accordance with the Design Responsibility Matrix incorporating Information Exchanges and Design Programme • Undertake third party consultations as required and any Research and Development aspects • Assist lead designer with preparation of stage Design Programme • Provide information for preparation of Cost Information and Project Strategies
Cost consultant	☐ ☐	• Update preliminary Cost Information • Assist lead designer with preparation of stage Design Programme
Construction lead	☐	• Update Construction Strategy
Contract administrator		N/A
Health and safety adviser	☐	• Update Health and Safety Strategy
All additional project roles	☐ ☐	• Liaise with project lead and lead designer as required • Provide information as set out in the Design Responsibility Matrix incorporating Information Exchanges in accordance with Design Programme

Stage 4

Technical Design

Project role		Tasks to be undertaken
All roles	☐ ☐	• Contribute to Health and Safety Strategy as required • Provide information for and contribute to contents of Project Execution Plan as required
Client and/or client adviser	☐ ☐	• Comment on Technical Design proposals as requested • Comment on updated Project Strategies as requested
Project lead	☐ ☐ ☐ ☐ ☐ ☐	• Monitor progress of developing design • Review updated Handover Strategy, Project Strategies and Risk Assessments with project team • Review and update Project Execution Plan • Comment on stage Design Programme • Manage change control process • Monitor and review progress and performance of project team
Lead designer	☐ ☐ ☐ ☐ ☐	• Review Technical Design proposals and Project Strategies as they progress and integrate the design work of specialist subcontractors in accordance with Design Programme • Update Sustainability Strategy and Maintenance and Operational Strategy with input from project team as required • Prepare stage Design Programme in conjunction with other design team members • Monitor and review progress and performance of design team • Liaise with specialist subcontractors as necessary
Architect	☐ ☐ ☐ ☐ ☐ ☐	• Prepare architectural Technical Design in accordance with the Design Responsibility Matrix incorporating Information Exchanges, Design Programme and comments from lead designer • Submit Building Regulations submission (Building Warrant in Scotland) • Undertake third party consultations as required and conclude any Research and Development aspects • Assist lead designer with preparation of stage Design Programme • Provide information for update of Project Strategies • Liaise with specialist subcontractors as necessary
Building services engineer	☐ ☐ ☐ ☐ ☐	• Prepare building services Technical Design in accordance with the Design Resonsibility Matrix incorporating Information Exchanges, Design Programme and comments from lead designer • Undertake third party consultations as required and any Research and Development aspects • Assist lead designer with preparation of stage Design Programme • Provide information for update of Cost Information and Project Strategies • Liaise with specialist subcontractors as necessary
Civil and structural engineer	☐ ☐ ☐ ☐ ☐	• Prepare Technical Design for structural design in accordance with the Design Responsibility Matrix incorporating Information Exchanges and Design Programme • Undertake third party consultations as required and any Research and Development aspects • Assist lead designer with preparation of stage Design Programme • Provide information for preparation of Cost Information and Project Strategies • Liaise with specialist subcontractors as necessary
Cost consultant	☐ ☐	• Update preliminary Cost Information • Assist lead designer with preparation of stage Design Programme
Construction lead	☐	• Prepare Construction Strategy
Contract administrator	☐	• Prepare Building Contract, agree with contractor and arrange completion
Health and safety adviser	☐	• Update Health and Safety Strategy, including statutory requirements
All additional project roles	☐ ☐	• Liaise with project lead and lead designer as required • Provide information as set out in the Design Responibility Matrix incorporating Information Exchanges in accordance with Design Programme

Where it is appropriate to allocate an additional task(s) to a specific role(s) or to move a task to a different role, the template available at www.ribaplanofwork.com/toolbox can be used to add these tasks.

Stage 5

Construction

Project role		Tasks to be undertaken
All roles	☐ ☐	• Contribute to Health and Safety Strategy as required • Provide information for and contribute to contents of Project Execution Plan as required
Client and/or client adviser	☐	• Respond to queries raised by project lead or contract administrator as required
Project lead	☐ ☐ ☐ ☐	• Manage implementation of Handover Strategy • Review and update Project Execution Plan as required • Comment on Construction Programme • Monitor and review progress and performance of project team
Lead designer	☐ ☐	• Carry out site inspections and review against specification and Construction Programme • Assist design team members with responses to Design Queries from site related to coordination or integration
Architect	☐ ☐ ☐	• Carry out site inspections and review against specification and Construction Programme • Respond to Design Queries from site as they arise • Prepare 'As-constructed' Information
Building services engineer	☐ ☐ ☐	• Carry out site inspections and review against specification and Construction Programme • Respond to Design Queries from site as they arise • Prepare 'As-constructed' Information
Civil and structural engineer	☐ ☐ ☐	• Carry out site inspections and review against specification and Construction Programme • Respond to Design Queries from site as they arise • Prepare 'As-constructed' Information
Cost consultant	☐	• Prepare valuations in accordance with Building Contract
Construction lead	☐	• Update Construction Strategy
Contract administrator	☐ ☐ ☐	• Administrate Building Contract • Manage change control process • Coordinate site inspections
Health and safety adviser	☐ ☐	• Update Health and Safety Strategy • Review 'As-constructed' Information
All additional project roles	☐ ☐	• Liaise with project lead as required • Provide information as set out in the Design Responsibility Matrix incorporating Information Exchanges

Where it is appropriate to allocate an additional task(s) to a specific role(s) or to move a task to a different role, the template available at www.ribaplanofwork.com/toolbox can be used to add these tasks.

Stage 6

Handover and Close Out

Project role		Tasks to be undertaken
All roles	☐	
Client and/or client adviser	☐	• Respond to queries in relation to handover of building as required
Project lead	☐ ☐ ☐	• Manage tasks listed in Handover Strategy • Manage updating of 'As-constructed' Information • Monitor and review progress and performance of project team
Lead designer	☐ ☐	• Undertake tasks listed in Handover Strategy • Review updated 'As-constructed' Information
Architect	☐ ☐	• Undertake tasks listed in Handover Strategy • Update 'As-constructed' Information in accordance with Design Responsibility Matrix incorporating Information Exchanges
Building services engineer	☐ ☐	• Undertake tasks listed in Handover Strategy • Update 'As-constructed' Information in accordance with Design Responsibility Matrix incorporating Information Exchanges
Civil and structural engineer	☐ ☐	• Undertake tasks listed in Handover Strategy • Update 'As-constructed' Information in accordance with Design Responsibility Matrix incorporating Information Exchanges
Cost consultant	☐ ☐	• Undertake tasks listed in Handover Strategy • Agree final account in accordance with Building Contract
Construction lead	☐ ☐	• Undertake tasks listed in Handover Strategy • Manage preparation and issue of 'As-constructed' Information by specialist subcontractors in accordance with Design Responsibility Matrix incorporating Information Exchanges
Contract administrator	☐ ☐	• Advise on the resolution of defects • Conclude administration of Building Contract
Health and safety adviser	☐	• Review Project Information
All additional project roles	☐ ☐	• Liaise with project lead as required • Provide information as set out in the Design Responsibility Matrix incorporating Information Exchanges

Where it is appropriate to allocate an additional task(s) to a specific role(s) or to move a task to a different role, the template available at www.ribaplanofwork.com/toolbox can be used to add these tasks.

Stage 7

In Use

Project role		Tasks to be undertaken
All roles	☐	
Client and/or client adviser	☐	• Undertake tasks listed in Handover Strategy
Project lead	☐ ☐	• Manage completion of tasks listed in Handover Strategy • Manage updating of Project Information
Lead designer	☐ ☐	• Undertake tasks listed in Handover Strategy • Review updated Project Information Information
Architect	☐	• Undertake tasks listed in Handover Strategy
Building services engineer	☐	• Undertake tasks listed in Handover Strategy
Civil and structural engineer	☐	• Undertake tasks listed in Handover Strategy
Cost consultant	☐	• Undertake tasks listed in Handover Strategy
Construction lead	☐	• Undertake tasks listed in Handover Strategy
Contract administrator		N/A
Health and safety adviser	☐	• Undertake tasks listed in Handover Strategy
All additional project roles	☐	• Undertake tasks listed in Handover Strategy

Note: Services required as part of ongoing (long-term) Stage 7 duties are not listed.
It is anticipated that these will be included in separate professional services contracts or operating contracts.

Where it is appropriate to allocate an additional task(s) to a specific role(s) or to move a task to a different role, the template available at www.ribaplanofwork.com/toolbox can be used to add these tasks.

Index